THE FIRST BLACK MAYOR
OF TERRY, MS

A Memoir

R O D E R I C K   T.   N I C H O L S O N

authorHOUSE®

AuthorHouse™
1663 Liberty Drive
Bloomington, IN 47403
www.authorhouse.com
Phone: 1 (800) 839-8640

Published by AuthorHouse   11/18/2016

ISBN: 978-1-5246-5091-9 (sc)
ISBN: 978-1-5246-5090-2 (e)

Library of Congress Control Number: 2016919256

Print information available on the last page.

Acknowledgements

There have been many persons who have been supportive, encouraging, and inspiring both in my administration as Mayor and in the writing of these memoirs. First and foremost, I would like to acknowledge and thank my wife JoAnn, daughters Vanessa and Melissa, and son Roderick Michael. They are the ones who endured my absences, listened to my complaints, and shared their husband and father with the Town of Terry for almost 15 years. They continued to express their love and support during my unfortunate brief incarceration. And for that, I am truly grateful. I thank God that through this we continue to be a supportive and loving family. My kids reinforce the saying that "good fruit doesn't come from a bad tree."

I would like to thank my wife's family, the Ransburgs of Canton, MS, for their love and support that they have shown our entire family over the years, and these past couple of years especially.

I would like to thank my sisters, Ms. Priscilla Nicholson and Mrs. Brenda N. Dube who traveled from Texas to Mississippi to offer their moral and other support in my time of need. I would also like to thank my other sister, Sharon D. Nicholson, for her heartfelt letter of support that she sent on my behalf to the Rankin County Circuit Court. As miserable as this time was for me, our late parents would be proud to see us siblings come together in a time of need and support one another as they did for me.

I would also like to thank Danny and Sylvia McDavid. For more than ten years, Sylvia served for years as the town's Deputy Clerk and Water Clerk. Sylvia shared my vision of high standards and excellence and did the lion's share of the work that resulted in significant improvements made in our mandatory annual water quality evaluations with the MS Department of Health. Her husband Danny McDavid helped the town countless times pro bono with many IT issues with our Terry Water Service software.

I would like to acknowledge the Terry Public Works Director Mr. James Green for his accommodating disposition and his entire staff for their sincere desire to help make Terry the best that it could be. Mr. Green is worth his weight in gold for his contribution to the Town of Terry and to me as Mayor.

I would like to thank the entire Terry Police Department for their professionalism, dedication, and unequivocal support that they gave me while I served as Mayor.

I would like to collectively thank the Friends of Terry organization for their support and contributions to the Town. An integral part of their fundraising efforts in Town is their dinner theater for which they are renown throughout the State of Mississippi and beyond. I affectionately take credit for their efforts although the only thing that I have done was preside as Mayor over the town in which this group operates.

I would like to thank Reverend Lennell McGee and Ms. Bertha Cooper. Reverend McGee was one of the first persons to encourage me to run for Mayor. Both Reverend McGee and Ms. Cooper have remained loyal supporters throughout all of my trials and tribulations as Mayor. They are some of the few persons that I would consider friends for life.

I would like to thank Messrs. Karl Ulrich and James Alexander. I met these gentlemen more than 30 years ago when I lived in metropolitan Chicago, and they have been friends since that time. Both gentlemen have been supportive over the years and have given me good advice in the writing of these memoirs.

I would like to acknowledge the support of Darryl and Wanda Bowen, Michael and Betty Early, Louis and Shirley Gibbs, Warren and Loretta Brown, Christopher and Annie Baker, Larry and Pamela Mann and the many of my neighbors in the Southfork Estates subdivision of Terry, MS for their political, spiritual, and other support shown during my family's trials and tribulations with the State of Mississippi. The people here in Southfork are really a special lot.

I would like to thank Drs. Charles and Priscilla Robinson for their friendship and support over the years that we have both lived in Terry, MS. They truly epitomize a friend in need is a friend indeed. Thank you Charles and Priscilla for being there for my family and myself when we needed it most.

I would like to acknowledge Hinds County District 2 Board of Supervisor Darrel McQuirter for his faith, support, both political and otherwise over the years. I cannot thank you enough for all that you have done. Hinds County and Mississippi needs more people with the spirit, knowledge, and temperament of Supervisor McQuirter.

I would like to include in my acknowledgements Messrs. Michael Shannon (Pearl, MS); Joseph Peyton (Gulfport, MS); and Tony Elliott (New Orleans, LA). Though brief, my incarceration was a most miserable and humiliating experience. These gentlemen offered words of encouragement, shared their respective life stories and demonstrated an understanding that surprised, impressed and sustained me. I wish them the best, and hopefully one day I'll hear from them again.

And finally, I would like to thank my "yard men", Messrs. Clifton Jackson and Monroe Powell for their hard work and attentive detail to the maintenance of my property over these past 15 years. Prior to my becoming Mayor, I insisted on doing my own lawn maintenance because I just didn't think that anyone would give my lawn the care that I did. However, I truly feel that Mr. Jackson and Mr. Powell's care of my lawn have exceeded anything that I could have done on my own. And I thank them sincerely for their service.

Introduction/Foreword

For more than 10 years, I served as Mayor of the Town of Terry, MS. Terry is a small town of about 1,200 persons in central Mississippi just off of Interstate Route 55. I had the distinction of being the town's first African American Mayor. During my 10+ years as Mayor, there were a number of positive things that were accomplished. This includes the construction of a new, award winning city hall building, a municipal library, construction of a combination fire station-public works building, rehabilitation of both the major north-south and east-west streets, significant improvements in and expansions of the municipal water and sewer infrastructure, improvements in the town's fire insurance rating, and jumpstarting economic development in this small town with a limited tax base. These are things that any Mayor would strive to achieve. In my opinion, what makes these accomplishments remarkable is when you consider how stagnant this town was for so many years prior to my administration as Mayor.

This progress was the result of long hours and very hard work. As I look back upon my years of service, there were many persons of good will and from all walks of life who helped and encouraged me along the way. At the same time, there was a sinister, negative undercurrent present in the culture and fabric of both the town and state. Race continues to permeate every aspect of life in Mississippi. Class differences are present although to a lesser extent. And both have stymied Mississippi from reaching her full potential.

Some statistics indicate that some 80% of people in Mississippi were born here. This might explain why outsiders are looked upon with a degree of suspicion regardless of how long they may have lived here and how committed they are to making positive contributions to this state. Both black and white cultures tend to be tribal, provincial, and closed. As an African American Mayor, I was constantly confronted with issues impacted by race, class, and navigating the often tricky nuances of Southern culture in the execution of the office of the Mayor.

One of Mississippi's greatest assets is her people. Simultaneously, one of her greatest liabilities is also her people. On the surface, this may seem like a contradiction, but upon deeper examination it really is not. You see, the people who are the assets and those who are the liability represent two distinct groups. And these groups are not necessarily divided along racial or political lines.

During the mid-19th century, Mississippi was part of a Confederacy at war with the United States over the issue of slavery. During the 1960's, Mississippi was at loggerheads with the much of the nation regarding extending voting, public accommodations, and education rights to African Americans. Even today, Mississippi continues to be a state engaged in a civil war with herself.

However, there is an emerging, progressive vein of people within the state from all demographics who are painfully aware and ashamed of the state's past and who desperately want the state to live up to its full potential and operate on parity with the rest of our nation. While at the same time, there is a group of persons who feels most comfortable preserving and living in the past oblivious that change is inevitable. These factions must be reconciled if Mississippi is to ever achieve consistent, sustainable progress in areas of education, employment, economic progress, and retention of our best and brightest individuals. A state cannot move forward if entire demographics of persons are disenfranchised.

The purpose of this book is to describe both the accomplishments of my administration as well as the racial, cultural, political, and other obstacles that I faced as Mayor. My accomplishments as Mayor reflect the tremendous potential and opportunity that Mississippi represents. The obstacles that confronted me also mirror the fundamental problems that have resulted in Mississippi consistently being on the bottom (and deservedly so) in most national rankings. It is my hope that by making a sincere attempt to more fully describe the problems in the state that we can all work toward a solution.

I had to think long and hard about writing a memoir about my experiences as the first African American Mayor of the Town of Terry, MS. As an African American, I think that it's especially important that we produce a recordation of our history because if we don't, that history will assuredly be written by someone else. For my legacy as Mayor, it's important that people hear from me about my experiences and thoughts. This is my story, my account, and in my words.

My Background

I was born April 26, 1957 in St. Mary's Infirmary in St. Louis, MO, to Prince and Dorothy Ruffin Nicholson. I am the third of five children which includes three sisters, a brother, and me. I grew up in E. St. Louis, IL. I also have a half-sister from my father's first marriage. Both my parents are deceased, and all of my siblings currently survive.

At the time that I grew up, E. St. Louis, IL was a working class predominantly African American community. Over the years, a lot of negativity has been said about E. St. Louis. Much of the situation is complicated and similar to some of the negativity that is spoken about the State of Mississippi. Nonetheless, the time that I grew up in E. St. Louis, IL (in the 60's and 70's); I remember it being a mostly positive experience.

It wasn't the South, but I was certainly aware of racism. There weren't "Jim Crow" laws that openly prohibited blacks from receiving services. But I was aware that white people generally didn't like living around African Americans. Both neighborhoods that I grew up in were initially integrated, but slowly, eventually all the whites moved away.

Despite that, I would say the K-12 education that I received was second to none. And my family as well as the community that I grew up in put an importance on education. Fortunately for me, I always did fairly well in school. I was salutatorian of 691 students of the E. St. Louis Senior High School graduating class of June 1975.

In the fall of 1975, I enrolled at the University of Illinois at Urbana-Champaign. Perhaps like a lot of students, I came to college not really knowing what I wanted to do. During my first year, I was an Undecided Pre-Med major. I then switched over to Chemical Engineering. During my junior year of college and after taking organic chemistry, I decided that I would switch my major again to Civil Engineering. I graduated with a

Bachelor of Science Degree in Civil Engineering with a double minor in Transportation Engineering and Environmental Engineering in May 1981.

I didn't have the perspective then as I do now about things such as race and class in America. I guess that my conscious awareness of these issues began in college. The community that I grew up in was predominantly working class African American. In 1975, the University of Illinois had more than 35,000 students and was 99.9% white. One can imagine the cultural shock and adjustment that I as an African American had to undergo when I went to a majority white college. Back in those days, there was no discussion of diversity. However, in comparison to Mississippi, I would say that the University of Illinois was more liberal politically. University of Illinois was a land grant institution, and many of their academic programs had a reputation for excellence and were among the top national rankings. The engineering programs especially were extremely rigorous and considered on par with other higher education institutions such as Massachusetts Institute of Technology (MIT), University of California at Berkeley, and Stanford University to name a few.

If I had to compare any of the colleges in Mississippi to the University of Illinois, I would have to say that Mississippi State University is somewhat similar. Mississippi State is also a land grant university with a number of agriculture-related programs, and it has a predominantly working class student body. However, I would say that Mississippi State University is decidedly more conservative than the University of Illinois at Urbana-Champaign. My oldest daughter graduated from Mississippi State with a Bachelors Degree in International Business with a specialty in Spanish. My son currently attends Mississippi State University and is pursuing a degree in Poultry Science with a specialty in Business Management.

In 1981 (the year that I graduated from the University of Illinois), there were a total of 8,836 Bachelor Degrees granted by the University of Illinois. The total number of Bachelor's Degrees granted in all the engineering disciplines was 1,284. Of this 1,284 engineering degrees granted, only 11 engineering degrees were granted to African American males. Essentially, this means that less than one percent (0.0086) of the engineering degrees granted by the College of Engineering at the University of Illinois at Urbana-Champaign in 1981 was to African American males.

By contrast to today, in 2015, the total school enrollment at the University of Illinois Urbana campus had increased to 44,087 students. In 2015, the University of Illinois awarded 12,391 total Bachelor Degrees which included 1,650 engineering degrees. Of this 1,650 total, 16 degrees were awarded to African American males, or (0.0097). When you compare the percentages, the percentages of African American males receiving undergraduate degrees at the University of Illinois has remained statistically unchanged (less than one per cent) in the more than 35 years since I received my undergraduate degree.[1]

It's my speculation that these numbers and percentages at the University of Illinois are representative of colleges and universities across the country as well within the engineering field. The vast majority of engineering graduates then and now are white males. And although white females are a minority in the field of engineering, their numbers (then and now) exceed the numbers of minority males. There are even fewer minority female engineers than minority male engineers (then and now).

---

[1]   Information obtained from the Division of Management Information (DMI) – University of Illinois at Urbana-Champaign (2016).

Coming to Chicago, IL

   In January 1982, I accepted a job as a Civil Engineer with District One of the Illinois Department of Transportation in Schaumburg, IL. Schaumburg is a suburb of Chicago, also located in Cook County about 35 miles northwest of downtown Chicago Loop. I look back upon both my professional and personal experience at IDOT and living in northwest suburban Chicago as being one of the most golden periods of my adult life. There were a number of other young people at IDOT. Some were also graduates from the University of Illinois or other colleges and universities, while others came directly into the workforce from high school or by way of community college. It was in Chicago that I also met the woman who would eventually become my wife.

Coming to Mississippi

I came to Mississippi in mid-1986 from Chicago, IL because I married a girl from Mississippi who often spoke about how she absolutely loved Mississippi. She is the former JoAnn Ransburg. We met in Chicago, IL and shortly after we married in 1985, she expressed a desire to leave Chicago and come back to Mississippi to be a married couple and perhaps start a family. I really liked living in northwest suburban Chicago. But Chicago was neither of our original homes (I was raised in East Saint Louis, IL). I was young, in love, and certainly more adventurous than I am now. And equally naïve.

Within a year of us being married, I found a job at the U.S. Army Corps of Engineers in Vicksburg, MS. We were excited, and I took the job sight unseen. I reported to work in July 1986. We lived in an apartment in Jackson, MS. It was a very nice 2 bedroom apartment just east of the Metrocenter Mall. I commuted daily from Jackson to Vicksburg.

Clinton, MS

I was really impressed with how much more affordable (and often newer) the properties were in Jackson, MS at the time in comparison to those in Chicago. In late 1986, we purchased a nearly new 1,600 square feet, 4 bedroom, 2 bath informal plan home in Clinton, MS. Shortly thereafter we got settled in our new home, we discovered we were expecting. Our first child was born at the end of October 1987. As a matter of fact, all three of our children were born in Clinton, MS as well.

Clinton was (and is) a really nice community. Both my wife and I have always been big advocates of education, and the Clinton school system was known to be among one of the best in the area.

However, one thing that I noticed in our neighborhood was how it seemed that almost every week in my neighborhood, one house or another was going on the market for sale. (Our home actually was a repossession that had gone into foreclosure from the previous owners.) Eventually, I realized that what was happening was a pattern of white flight in our neighborhood. Sadly, a number of these persons simply walked away from their homes. Growing up in E. St. Louis, IL our family had experienced the same pattern of "white flight", and I knew that this could spell trouble in a number of ways. And eventually it did. Often, when people simply walk away from their homes for these reasons, the banks will allow the house to be sold for considerably less than traditional market value. This often allows a family into a neighborhood that they normally wouldn't be considered for. The problems often result when the newcomers either can't or don't want to afford the associated costs which include utilities, taxes, homeowner association fees, and general upkeep. It isn't necessarily a black/white thing, but often the newer, (and most often African American) families end up bearing the burden of these circumstances. And you have a group of homeowners ill-equipped financially or mentally ready to assume responsibilities associated with home ownership.

Madison, MS

In the mid to late 1990's, there was a period of political and racial unrest and increase in crime in Jackson, MS. It was mostly whites fleeing Jackson for the suburbs in Rankin and Madison Counties. However, many African Americans who could afford to leave the City of Jackson began to leave as well. There was an exodus north out of Jackson to Madison and east into Rankin County. At this time, I had lived in Mississippi for about 10 years and so had developed my own impression of the prominence of race relations in just about everything in Mississippi. We considered moving again, but I expressed to my wife my concerns about getting into another "white flight" situation. But Madison was then and even today is considered a more progressive community. And although Madison is a predominantly white community, there were Black families in almost every subdivision and neighborhood.

Although we had a very nice home in Madison, I could never feel totally comfortable there. I like to think of myself as progressive in my outlook. However, Madison was perhaps a bit too class conscious for my taste. As anywhere, some people were friendly, some decidedly more cool. At the time we lived in Madison, there was a phenomenon of "equity building" among many homeowners. Some of these homeowners would live in a home for as little as 6 months to a year, sell their home at a profit (Madison properties had significant appreciation prior to the 2008 financial crash), take those profits and move to a nicer, larger home. I don't think that it was necessarily racist as in white flight. But this phenomenon did contribute to a very unstable neighborhood environment. We lived in Madison for 3-1/2 years. From there, we decided to purchase acreage property and build our dream home.

Terry, MS

We looked around for available land in Madison County, but it was way too expensive for us. So we eventually settled on a 3-1/2 acre parcel on the north side of the small community of Terry located in the far southern portion of Hinds County. This was an African American development. Initially, I was against it because I was so far out. But it had very good access to the interstate. By this time, I understood and had resigned myself to accept this unspoken "sense of place" in Mississippi. Most blacks stay in black neighborhoods, and whites did the same. And I'm not going to pick on the whites necessarily. The blacks seemed equally that way as well. And besides, even I could tell that I wouldn't be doing myself any favors by deliberately going against the grain by insisting on being "different" here in Mississippi.

Mississippi has always been somewhat uncomfortable for me culturally. And ironically, the Town of Terry even more so. It was a much smaller town. It had less than 1,000 persons when we moved here in late 1999. Actually, most of Mississippi is essentially rural. Culturally, what I really didn't like (but tolerated) was how nosy the people often were. I mean, I can understand anyone wanting to know their neighbors' names and basic information, but these people practically made you submit to an interview. But then, on the positive side, people did look out for you, and the Town of Terry was one place with a significant African American population and relatively low crime.

Terry did not (and still does not) offer many amenities or creature comforts such as a full-service grocery store, full-service banking, etc. You have to go to literally the next town north (Byram, MS) or beyond for full-service retail, medical, shopping, and even further for entertainment or other needs. In Terry, there is nobody to work on your car or fix a flat tire. We have a couple of gas station-convenience food stores. And most people seem to be content with that. This could be quite frustrating to a person such as me who by nature enjoys having creature comforts at one's fingertips.

Attending My First Board Meeting in Terry

I attended my first Town of Terry board meeting about 3-4 months after getting settled in our new home. I must say that I was unimpressed with the City Hall building. Actually, this building was the pits. The City Hall was an old converted white frame house. The building obviously hadn't been painted in years, and there was peeling paint all around the exterior. It's my understanding that one of the rooms in the City Hall also previously housed the local library. Speaking of which, the municipal library was a single-wide dilapidated trailer located down the street. The downtown area was about a block in length, and it was atrocious. Even today, I would never invite a visitor to our downtown area. It truly seemed so depressing and not reflective of any sort of community pride.

At any rate, the board room where most meetings and municipal court were held was ridiculously small. The Mayor, Town Clerk, and five Aldermen sat at two folding tables. The audience (it was barely sufficient seating for at most 10 persons) consisted of three persons present including me. The Board of Aldermen consisted of 3 white men, an African American male, and an African American female. The Mayor was a white guy.

I distinctly remember that only the Mayor and the Clerk had actual papers and documents to review. The minutes and any other information that the board needed was provided to them orally by the Mayor and Town Clerk. The board didn't receive minutes or any other documents. Until I came on the Board as an Alderman and requested hard copy documents for my review, the Board of Aldermen never previously received hard copy documents.

Running for Alderman

At the time that I attended my initial town meeting, I never envisioned or thought about being on any town board much less a Mayor. My purpose in attending was just to observe and become informed about the affairs of the town in which I resided. The then-Mayor impressed me as a rather gruff but otherwise OK individual. He did, however, seem to know how to take control of a situation. In retrospect, I'd have to say that he was a far better political animal than me.

After my initial board meeting attendance, I would continue to come to the board meetings periodically. Actually, the board meetings were so poorly attended by the public and the protocol so relaxed that they were more like conversations than meetings. After a short while, I got to know all of the board members. Also, I could tell that there was some tension between the then Mayor and both of the black Aldermen. At the time, I didn't know any of them well, and frankly, I didn't really see it as my concern whatever their personality dynamics were. However, one of the white Alderman and the Mayor gave off a friendly vibe to me. I later discovered that elections were coming up for all the Board, and both gentlemen were running for the Mayor's position. This could explain their friendliness that I earlier described. I believe that eventually either this alderman or the incumbent Mayor sent word through one of the town staff to inquire whether I would be interested in running for a seat on the Board of Aldermen.

It's interesting to me as an outsider, a transplant, about this Southern cultural phenomenon about how one often indirectly inquires through someone else. I would later see that a lot of business and interpersonal communications among Southerners is often conducted this way.

After some thought on this offer, I decided to run. It was flattering that I, this relative newcomer to town, was well enough received to be asked to join the town board. I decided to run, and I was elected to the Board of Aldermen. The incumbent Mayor was re-elected as well.

As I said earlier, for whatever reason, the incumbent Mayor never got along with either of the two other African American board members. I don't know why, but I assumed it was because the mayor was white, and they were black. During my term as an Alderman on the board, I personally witnessed on more than one occasion the mayor during board meetings tell both African American board members to "Shut up!" (and worse) and publicly fuss at and otherwise admonish them if they said something that he didn't agree with. I did think that this was rather rude. But strangely, both these African American aldermen would act like children and just sit there and sulk. Neither Alderman ever made much attempt to defend themselves against Mayor Pechloff when these situations occurred. In all fairness, the Mayor Pechloff would periodically admonish the other white board members as part of the discussions and disagreements regarding various town board matters as well.

And because of the open tension between the mayor and the other Black aldermen, I just figured that it would be a matter of time before the mayor would go off on me just as he had with the other board members. I kind of lived in fear and dread of this, and I sometimes pondered what I would do should I be publicly confronted in this way. However, this never happened in all my four years as an Alderman. This mayor and I actually had a decent professional relationship. Sometimes, I think that the fact that the former Mayor seemed to have more respect for me than the other African American aldermen may have contributed to the feelings of jealousy and disdain that they seemed to develop toward me during the more than ten years that I served as Mayor of the town.

Running for Mayor

The term that I served as an Alderman was in some ways interesting, but ultimately disappointing. On a number of occasions, one of the African American aldermen had publicly spoken about their desire to run for mayor. As the qualifying deadline approached to file for office, I personally encouraged both the other black aldermen to consider running. In the end, both declined to run for various reasons.

Years later, I think that although they may have long coveted occupying the position of mayor, they may have declined because they were afraid to run against a white incumbent. Another speculation that I have is that they may have felt they didn't have the temperament and/or want the headache to handle the responsibilities of mayor.

Ironically, about this same time, there began to be a slow, steady drum from some of the community folk pushing me to run for mayor. Actually, I do remember a relative of one of the white alderman put a large, homemade sign in their front yard encouraging me to run for Mayor. Prior to this, I never really seriously considered running for mayor. On two separate occasions, I was formally asked by several of the townsfolk to run, and both times I politely refused. The third time, various ones mentioned it to my wife, and she relayed the message and suggested that I just reconsider. Although it was with a degree of trepidation, but after some thought I did agree to run for the office of mayor. And like most small towns in Mississippi, the mayor ran as an Independent; that is with no affiliation to any political party (such as Democrat or Republican).

Essentially, the candidates for Mayor were the incumbent Mayor and me. Although the town had never had an African American Mayor, I didn't initially look at this as very radical or really even consider the historical significance in all this. However, there were others in the community who saw nothing but the racial implications, and they didn't hesitate to let me know.

For instance, some of the African American clergy were nervous about this and sent word through others *(this Southern way of doing things in an oblique fashion)* requesting that I not ever come to church on Sunday and even think about mentioning anything to anyone about the election at church.

I found this to be a bit ironic and hypocritical because it was (and still is) a very accepted Southern tradition that whenever you wanted to introduce yourself to people or get some message out that it was quite accepted that you would either pay a personal visit or send a handwritten notice to the various churches to be included in the announcements that were read each Sunday.

There was one African American church in particular that I had contacted and asked whether I could speak to those present either before or at the conclusion of their weekly Wednesday evening Bible study. Although this deacon in charge did eventually allow me to speak, did he ever give me such a runaround! I've never been the most observant when it comes to interpersonal communications, and reflecting back on these experiences over time I can more clearly see that some of the unspoken nuances of Southern culture.

There was another African American church that I had contacted to come by at a mutually agreeable time and day (not a Sunday) to speak to their congregation about my platform and some things that I was interested in doing should I be elected Mayor. A day before I was scheduled to meet, I received a call from some guy who identified himself as a member of this church's deacon board. He sounded exasperated and troubled. He said that the deacons had had a meeting, and some had voiced concerns that it might be too controversial for me to speak at their church. I asked what kind of controversy would my speaking create, and he just repeated his earlier statement. I thanked him politely for at least considering my request and just left it at that.

Looking back, it's likely that the "controversy" that they felt uncomfortable about was the fact that I was an African American running against a white incumbent for the position of Mayor.

It's a bit ironic that about two years into my first term as Mayor that I was contacted by this same church inviting me to one of their annual church events. They indicated that as Mayor that I would have special seating and would be given an allotment of time for remarks as I saw fit. This is the same church that previously thought my presence was too "controversial". I informed the church leadership that I would be unavailable to attend.

One of the white churches in Terry also sent word through an intermediary that I should absolutely not consider coming to their church politicking. Subsequently however, I was later contacted by a number of their members indicating that they absolutely were going to support me in the Mayoral election. To this day, I don't know how I should interpret their collective action. Perhaps it may have been their sincere desire to maintain a separation of church and state.

Now as nervous as some churches may have been to allow my presence, there were others who fully embraced me and were welcoming from day one. It's only in writing about my experiences I can see how provincial some of the thinking in this small town was and to some degree continues to be.

Despite all of the underlying tensions surrounding the election, there was some excitement from both black and white communities about my running for Mayor. Looking back, it wasn't a particularly ugly election. I had before never run for Mayor, so I had nothing to compare this experience to. Until I ran, the town never even had much of an election because there just wasn't that much interest in political office. And in my opinion, the sorry state of the town was reflective of that.

I didn't have a true election committee per se. I don't even think that I solicited or received any contributions. I paid my own expenses for flyers and what few political signs that I had out of my own pocket. I got on my computer and wrote up some basic information about myself and some of the things that I hoped to accomplish should I be elected. When I needed additional copies to distribute, I took my "template" flyers to Kinkos Copy Center in north Jackson for reproduction.

I was really surprised that a number of the older, white persons were very supportive of me. Now, it wasn't that I wasn't aware of the tensions between the white and black communities down South. Perhaps, it may have been because of my background as an engineer that people embraced my running for Mayor. Maybe they felt that my professional background could be beneficial in helping the town address some of its dire infrastructure needs.

It was my initial impression that most of the current board was in support of my running for Mayor. However, looking back on the events, I now feel that wasn't exactly the case. With my running, I think that the African American establishment of the community could hope to unseat the white mayor without personally having to get their hands dirty in the process. It's also possible that the other African American board members may have been unwilling to run because they didn't want to give up their coveted seats on the board and/or didn't feel that they could successfully unseat a white incumbent.

Looking back on the entire experience, I think that the local African American establishment's plan was to use me to unseat the incumbent white mayor, and that I would be only a one-term Mayor. To the establishment, I was dispensable. And then the black establishment families would then run their candidate of choice and then come in and take over. And that may very well have been a workable plan. However, nobody ever took the time to inform me about the plan and/or whether I would be agreeable to be a part of it. In retrospect, I feel that I was an unwitting pawn in their political game.

In my opinion, this behavior continues to hurt Blacks especially. For good or bad, people often act out what has been played out in front of them. Perhaps the black establishment families witnessed and experienced this type of treatment from the racist whites who were in power before them. And perhaps, too, this is the only way that they felt that they could gain political strength and control. Or maybe, this is just the way politics works. Period. It's all so very sad.

I still find it absolutely amazing how some Black people to this day remain reticent to stand up to white people (just because they are white), yet these same people can behave like gangsters, thugs, and bullies in taking from and manipulation of their own people. Perhaps this is a behavior that may have been a survival mechanism during slavery and/or the Jim Crow era. But the world has moved on, and this is but a dysfunctional behavior that is of no benefit to anyone in a progressive society.

More often than not, in most small towns, the office of Mayor is Independent. That is, with no Democrat, Republican, or other political party affiliation. In all the more than ten years that I served the town as Mayor, I ran and served as an Independent. Also in small towns in Mississippi, the Board of Aldermen are all at-large. In other words, the top five vote getters for Board seats become the new Board.

This type of election of board members favors incumbents because they have a name recognition advantage. And candidates either backed by or related to the political establishment as is often the case have an advantage as well. In most small towns in Mississippi, the Board of Aldermen is not elected from nor do they politically represent specific sections or wards of town. A number of the current Board of Aldermen of Terry consists of relatives and/or persons who live in close proximity of one another. At-large election of an entire board can skew the representation of political ideas significantly. In other words, some political ideologies can monopolize a town while other parts of town have no direct political board representation at all.

On more than one occasion, I have personally observed municipalities throughout Mississippi that have greater than seventy-five percent African American population yet have an entirely white Board of Aldermen. Other issues may also be at play and contribute to facilitate such outcomes which include voter apathy and/or systemic disenfranchisement created by the court systems where a disproportionate number of African Americans have simply lost their right to vote and thus participate in the election process.

At any rate, the election was held the first Tuesday of June 2005. The election was uneventful, close, yet decisive. I remember being at City Hall shortly after the poll closed (we had only one polling location) and observed the municipal election commission manually tally the votes. After the votes had been counted and confirmed, I was declared the winner of the election contest and thus the new Mayor-elect. I do remember that there was some surprise and obvious discomfort by several of those present at my being elected. However, I didn't have any one specifically there for me as there often might be in the traditional type of post election. I didn't have an assembly of supporters there. This building was so small that it would hardly have accommodated such a group anyway. The current mayor was there also, and I do recall him being gracious. He shook my hand, congratulated me, and left shortly after the announcement.

I also left after a brief time and went directly home. My wife and kids were at home, and after I arrived at home, I told them that I had been elected as the new Town Mayor. In those days, there was so little interest in Terry that there wasn't even a news crew down in Terry to cover the event. My family was overjoyed with the news. There may have been a brief mention about my election on the local 10 o'clock news.

Over the next few days, I remember receiving e-mails of congratulations from various professional partners such as the Central MS Planning and Development District that I had previously worked with as an Alderman on the town's planning and zoning matters.

In the next several days, I also heard from several persons who did business with the Town. This would include people such as the lady who did our financial books to vendors who provided uniforms and other services to the town. I don't know what I actually expected the job of Mayor to be, but after a month or two, I could clearly see that it was a lot more than I expected, even for a small town. As an Alderman, I had never concerned myself with the specific day-to-day activities of the Mayor. My only recollection was that the previous Mayor wasn't at City Hall very often, and so it was my expectation that neither would I. However, I did have some new goals for the town. But I was incredibly naïve to think that they could happen just because I wanted them to.

It didn't take me long to come to the realization that the current staff was inadequate and didn't have the training or educational background to execute some of the things that I wanted. Still, I emphasized to the staff that I expected professionalism, competence, a high level of service to the public, and at the very least clean facilities with some sense of order and pride.

In my opinion, learning the job of Mayor was very similar to pursuing a college degree. In order to be an effective Mayor, there were so many areas that you needed to have proficient knowledge of. Including knowing the basics about various communities in town, and how things are put together, what the town's strengths and weaknesses were, and some of the predominant goals and hopes within each community and neighborhood.

Considering that I was also still learning about many of the unspoken nuances of Southern culture, I certainly had my work cut out for me.

I can remember so clearly as I was on my way to preside over my first meeting as Mayor that it dawned on me that I no longer vote but rather I am going to have to lay out the best case for the Board members with the hopes that they will buy into and support my vision and agenda for the town.

I took my responsibility as Mayor seriously. I was determined that I was going to get something done. But the problem was was that getting something done made it more difficult for my political adversaries to move me out of the position. During my first term as Mayor, I had formulated a record of accomplishment and eventual acceptance of the rank-and-file of both black and white communities. It was during my second term as Mayor that I believe that is when the personal ugliness and almost constant attempts to discredit and be contrary with everything I proposed and accomplished began.

In my opinion, one shouldn't just covet a political office just for the sake of occupying a position. I have a theory about why far too many African American communities seem to consistently lag and/or achieve lasting success when compared to other communities. It isn't that I think that Black people are somehow genetically inferior or otherwise similarly lacking. Because we are all Americans, our thoughts (both black and white) are shaped by the same culture. And as Americans, we all have the similar aspirations and thoughts.

However, the reality is that African Americans often have not been adequately prepared for success. And preparation often involves grueling, time consuming, and often thankless work. Because we are Americans and human, we all aspire for the same end product in however we define success. However, success is rarely instantaneous. Unfortunately, too many of us define "success" as what we think is either the most prestigious and/or easiest job. We as Americans are subconsciously taught to aspire to this.

Black communities and leadership often fall short because too often too many African Americans aspire to only ONE job with no real thoughtful consideration about whether we are qualified or have the temperament for this ONE job. Far too many African Americans fail to see that a successful community or undertaking is often comprised of MANY jobs that work in concert with one another. Because of this thinking, many of us end up coveting and fighting over one job while many other (equally valuable though perceived as less prestigious) jobs remain unfilled. A machine cannot properly operate unless all of its parts work in concert.

In addition, I think that the cumulative, corrosive effect of just living as a Black person in America can also erode our collective self-esteem is a significant contributing factor to our collective lack of community success as well. I truly do think that this may be a root cause of the jealousies that exist in our communities, churches, and other establishments and organizations. A wagon cannot move toward its destiny unless all the horses are yoked together. Again, this is my theory to explain why our communities consistently seem to operate below parity and often fail to attain the level of their true potential.

When I initially ran for Mayor, my platform was to build the town's infrastructure and provide a higher level of services to the town. I viewed my successful election as confirmation that this was the desire and mandate of the majority of the community.

However, I don't think that this was the motive of a small group of these politically connected African American establishment families. In retrospect, it's quite clear to me that the black establishment families weren't primarily concerned with moving the town forward because there were plenty of opportunities for them to accomplish that years ago long before I came onto the scene in town. As dogged and determined as they were to get me out of City Hall, they apparently didn't dare stand up to the whites who collectively ran things practically into the ground. After more than a decade of observation of the African American establishment in Terry, I believe this with all my heart.

As much as the Black community is lacking, and as much real work that needs to be done, there are plenty of things that need attention where just about anyone could fulfill a legitimate need without taking from someone else. From day one, my only agenda has been to move this town forward in any way that I could with the resources available to me. How could I have known any of this when I casually walked into that first town hall meeting more than 16 years ago?

Construction of a New City Hall

When I became Mayor, the City Hall was this dilapidated white frame house located on Railroad Avenue just south of the intersection of Cunningham and Railroad Avenues. Not only was this building in bad condition, it was very poorly maintained. The building was so dirty and nasty. I was literally afraid to sit down. I had visited City Hall on occasion when I was an alderman, but I had never actually been all the way through the building until I became Mayor. City Hall had only one bathroom that had low water pressure and in serious need of cleaning and maintenance. This place was a dump!

At my insistence, we did manage to clean the place up a few months after I began my term as Mayor. As much work as we completed, many problems remained. The building was poorly insulated. The roof was on the verge of collapse. Several of the windows were either broken and/or in need of caulking, and none were energy efficient. The building had window unit air conditioning that took almost an hour to make the place comfortable during our long summer season. (We had a policy of cutting all energy off on the weekends and/or when no one was in the building.) The Public Works Department was also housed at City Hall, and so the building constantly reeked of diesel fuel.

As this was an old building, it was built raised off the ground. In the crawl space underneath the building, a stray mother cat with a litter of kittens had taken up residence. I absolutely could not believe that people in modern times tolerated these kinds of conditions at their main building of business and service for their town. However, after about two weeks we were finally able to remove this cat family. We put some lattice around the skirt of the building to prevent another cat or other animal from resuming residence under City Hall.

The final straw of my trying to continue to renovate this building came one day when we were in the process of painting the building's exterior. The exterior of the building was wood slat material and had been neglected for so long that it took a solid week to manually scrape the chipped paint off. When the painters attempted to use a pressure washer to finish preparing the surface for priming and painting, water went through the boards into the building's interior. At this point, I realized that this building is beyond repair and recommended to the Board that we needed to explore other options regarding a City Hall building.

Description: Old Terry City Hall.
Source: Mayor Rod Nicholson

This picture of the old City Hall is actually an improvement over what I initially inherited as Mayor. In this picture, we have painted the building and placed a lattice skirt around the bottom to prevent stray animals from taking up residence beneath the City Hall building.

• Converting the Old Hotel to City Hall

There was an old, vacant building right next door to City Hall. It was owned by Mr. Joe Weston who also owned the Mercantile Hardware Store located just on the other side of the hotel. I might add that there was some long-standing feud between hotel owner Mr. Weston and the former mayor. My understanding was that through some technicality, the former mayor had forced the closing of this building and demanded that Mr. Weston comply with some local code to install a fire escape at the rear of the building. Mr. Weston refused, and to this day, the building remains vacant.

The hotel was a 3-story building. When I first became Mayor in 2005, it was still in fairly good condition although it did need some work. We talked to Mr. Weston about purchasing this property. Mr. Weston made a counter-offer to lease the building but was not interested in selling. I didn't think that it would be a good idea for the town to sink a significant amount of money needed for renovations into a building that we would never own.

- **Finding A Location For A New City Hall**

A significant portion of the town's main street (Cunningham Avenue) is located on 16th Section land. Essentially, this is land controlled by the school board that is available for lease but never fee simple ownership. At any rate, the town under a previous administration had already entered into a long-term lease with the Hinds County School Board for an oddly shaped piece of land bisected by Cunningham Avenue. On the north side of Cunningham was the Village Square Park. On the south side was the town's water tower. The location of this 16th Section land parcel was about a half-mile west of the Railroad Avenue location of the original City Hall building.

Because this parcel of land was on our main street, I began to think that this might be a good location for a town hall. In addition, the location was about 1/8th mile from the interstate. We had the land surveyed to confirm that it could meet the requirements for the proposed building as well as off-street parking. I then approached the local school board about whether they would have any objections to adding a City Hall to our existing lease, and they agreed.

- **Obtaining Funding for City Hall**

I desperately searched to secure funding for the City Hall building. And although there were a couple of sources that seemed promising, I quickly realized that I perhaps may have gotten the cart before the horse in this undertaking. When asked, I couldn't provide answers to such basic questions as to the size of the building that was needed, the expected cost, what municipal functions would the building expect to serve, etc.

In order to get answers to these questions, I spoke to a number of architects about putting together a plan. After Hurricane Katrina in 2005, most architects in Mississippi wanted a cost-plus contract for municipal construction projects. Under a cost-plus scenario, the architectural costs were based on a set fee plus a percentage of the actual construction costs (including cost overruns) rather than a set fee for their services. I could see that this could quickly become expensive and cost prohibitive. So, I continued to search for a quality architect with whom the town could have some more mutually agreeable terms.

Eventually, I met with an architect out of Ridgeland, MS. This building designer essentially designed my personal home when I lived in Madison, MS. I really liked the architectural style of his buildings. And after a good deal of convincing, he did agree to provide his services for a fixed fee. This is the part of being Mayor that I really enjoyed: putting together infrastructure projects. I guess coming from a Civil Engineering background, municipal infrastructure projects were kind of a natural extension for me.

I have to say working with an architect on my first municipal infrastructure project was a real joy. The architect insisted in coming down to the old City Hall and personally inspecting the existing City Hall building. During our initial meeting, the architect took a lot of notes and asked a lot of questions. Some of the questions he asked included what were my frustrations with the existing building and what things did I hope to have in the new building. Afterwards, he drove around the downtown area presumably so that the architect could get some idea of potential architecture styles that would be compatible with the other structures in the vicinity of the proposed city hall building.

We went through several draft layouts for the new building. Eventually, a draft plan was presented to the board for their input and approval. The next biggest challenge was to find either a low interest loan or grant funds to allow the town to pursue the construction of this much needed building. Despite the dire need, the Board was not in favor of incurring any debt to finance a new City Hall building.

- **Meeting With Leland Speed, Mississippi Development Authority**

At any rate, I had heard that Mr. Leland Speed was then the Executive Director of the Mississippi Development Authority and had a special interest in helping small towns with improvement projects and that he might be a good person to speak with. Had I truly known about Mr. Speed's background, I'm sure that I would have been much more intimidated about contacting him. I cannot believe that I had the nerve to call the offices of MDA, ask him to meet me in Terry to discuss the possibility of a City Hall building in Terry. But surprisingly, he agreed.

I met with Mr. Speed, gave him a tour of the town's existing, dilapidated city hall, and explained what I was trying to do. He seemed quite receptive to my ideas and the fact that we planned to relocate city hall to Cunningham Avenue as part of our main street revitalization. Mr. Speed indicated that the town perhaps could qualify for $150K under MDA's Small Municipalities grant program and encouraged me to submit a grant application. Several months later, much to my surprise and delight, the Town of Terry received a grant to fund the City Hall building.

In the meantime, I continued to work with the architect and presented a final plan to the board. This was my first term as Mayor. At the time, the whites comprised a majority of the board. There was already some push back from the white community against the construction of a new City Hall building, and these people were speaking mainly through the white aldermen on the board.

I would not learn until sometime after the building was complete that some of the African American Aldermen were not as supportive of a new city hall as I had originally thought. However, they didn't openly go against the proposal because: 1) They didn't think that it would ever happen, and 2) Because there was a white faction so openly against a new city hall that they (the African American board members) only pretended to be supportive just to piss the whites off. Such is the long, tumultuous history between whites and blacks in this small Southern town.

At any rate, I explained to those in opposition of constructing a new city hall building that we had worked on trying to improve the existing city hall building for more than a year, and the renovations were just becoming too cost prohibitive. The existing building had severe foundation issues, the roof was showing signs of literally beginning to cave in, the electrical system was obsolete and in need of complete replacement, the building insulation was poor to non-existent, and the cost to bring the exterior of the building to an acceptable standard was just too much. It would be far cheaper and would be more functional to just build a new building in lieu of rehabilitating the existing city hall. And I was able to just barely muster enough votes from the board to agree on a plan and submit for bids. Just barely.

- **Low Bid Received for City Hall Construction Project**

We received bids from several qualified contractors. The low bidder was from Mr. Thomas (Tommy) M. Harkins. Mr. Harkins is a volume residential and commercial builder in the metropolitan Jackson, MS area. He had also recently acquired several lots in Terry Park subdivision here in Terry and had a good reputation for building attractive, quality house plans.

One of my concerns about his bid price was that it was significantly lower than the other bids received. Having dealt with the bid process as an engineer in my professional career with the federal and state governments, I knew that this is a matter that may warrant additional investigation. My other concern that even with his low bid, it was more double than our original grant amount of $150K.

At any rate, I met with Mr. Harkins, told him that he was the apparent low bidder but because his bid was significantly less than the others, I had some concerns to ensure that the bid was also realistic and would yield the town a quality product. Mr. Harkins explained that as a volume builder that he could purchase materials at a discounted price. He went on to explain in addition to having a residential construction business that he and his family also has other businesses related to building construction and as such he was able to purchase from these businesses at a reduced cost. Mr. Harkins presented a portfolio of his work which included various subdivisions in which he had constructed the lion's share of the homes and other commercial buildings that Harkins Builders had constructed to ensure me that he was fully capable of providing a quality product.

I then explained to Mr. Harkins that even at the apparent low bid that this significantly exceeded our $150K grant funds available for this project.

However, I stated to Mr. Harkins that I was interested in proceeding with this project and that I planned to go back to MDA and/or seek other grant funding source for additional funds. Mr. Harkins got back with me a few days later and indicated that $150K could get us through the complete framing process (slab, framing, roof, installation of brick on the exterior, windows, and exterior doors). The advantage of this is that the building's structural integrity and interior would be protected from the elements should the additional funding not materialize as timely as we might hope. Ultimately, this proved to be a non-issue because the town worked with our state representatives to ensure that we received the additional funding to complete construction of our City Hall building.

Working on the construction of this building was an extremely time-consuming joy. I couldn't have asked for a better general contractor than Tommy Harkins. Because the town could not afford to hire a person to essentially serve as resident inspector and represent the town's interests on this project, I decided to take this job on myself. I desperately wanted this infrastructure project to be successful, and as a civil engineer I did have the skill set needed. I neither asked for nor received any compensation for my services to this project. And fortunately, this project was a success. This project came in ahead of schedule and under budget. It is a beautiful building, and it received the 2008 National Innovation Award for Small Towns.

However, that is not to say that we didn't have our crosses to bear and difficult moments that in my opinion were totally manufactured. Some board members were quite difficult and presented obstacles to deliberately negatively impact the progress schedule.

As difficult as some aldermen were during the construction of the city hall building, it was a different story on the day of Open House. I remember this one alderwoman who had been so obstinate was the first one to show the news media and any of the other local leadership around the new building. I must say that I was surprised and delighted at her complete turnaround. Months later, I reminded her about how she had been so obstinate and difficult during the construction process and how she seemed to change at the Open House. At first she hesitated, and then she broke down crying and said how sorry she was about her previous actions. From that day forward, she was one of my staunchest supporters.

The other alderman in opposition was another story. I believe that he was the only alderman who refused to attend the Open House for the new City Hall building. When we had our first meeting at the new City Hall building, he simply refused to sit with the other aldermen although he was present at the meeting. Shortly thereafter, he submitted his letter of resignation from the board.

Description: The New Terry City Hall building.
Source: Central MS Planning & Development District; Jackson, MS

This replaced our old City Hall building. It was actually in a better location on Cunningham Avenue (our main east-west street). Although so many people fought this proposal, all grew to be supportive of this building.

NADO news release
NATIONAL ASSOCIATION OF DEVELOPMENT ORGANIZATIONS

400 North Capitol Street, NW, Suite 390, Washington, DC 20001
Tel: (202) 624-7806 • Email: info@nado.org • Website: www.nado.org
For Immediate Release: October 7, 2008
Contact: Zanetta Doyle, NADO Communications Manager

Central Mississippi Planning and Development District Receives National Association of Development Organization's 2008 Innovation Award

WASHINGTON, DC – The Central Mississippi Planning & Development District in Jackson, Mississippi received a 2008 Innovation Award from the National Association of Development Organizations (NADO) for its Terry Town Hall.

NADO is a Washington, DC-based association that promotes programs and policies that strengthen local governments, communities and economies through regional cooperation, program delivery and comprehensive strategies. The association's Innovation Awards program recognizes regional development organizations and partnering organizations for improving the economic and community competitiveness of our nation's regions and local communities. Award winners will be showcased during NADO's 2008 Annual Training Conference, October 3-7 in Anchorage, Alaska.

"For more than 20 years, NADO's Innovation Awards Program has provided a unique opportunity to showcase thousands of creative and cutting-edge projects like Terry Town Hall, which have been integral in preserving and advancing the economic growth and sustainability of our nation's regions. This recognition only further emphasizes the continued need for regional development organizations and their critical role in promoting economic development for the country's rural and small metropolitan communities," said NADO President Leanne Mazer, executive director of the Tri-County Council for Western MD in Cumberland, Maryland.

###

Founded in 1967, the National Association of Development Organizations (NADO) provides advocacy, education, networking and research for the national network of 540 regional development organizations. NADO members provide professional, programmatic and technical assistance to over 2,300 counties and 15,000 municipalities.

Description: Award Press Release of City Hall.
Source: Town of Terry, MS

Establishment of Cedarstone Subdivision in Terry, MS

Shortly after I became mayor, a couple of local developers approached the board to develop a vacant parcel of land for subdivision development. This was an approximately 33-acre parcel of vacant land nestled between Utica Street and Morgan Drive in the near north side of Terry. I told the board that I didn't have any problems with the developers' proposal. However, I did caution them that I fully expected them to include in their development infrastructure such as streets, water, sewer, gas, and electricity before the town would accept maintenance after subdivision completion.

About a month later, I was informed that there would be a new developer of this subdivision. I didn't know these new developers personally, but I did know that they had developed a number of properties north of Terry in Byram, MS. Essentially, they seemed to be quality brick starter homes. What really impressed me was that the planned subdivision in Terry would have all underground utilities. This was in synch with what I felt the town needed.

However, one problem that we had was the proposed lot size for Cedarstone subdivision. Our newly adopted zoning ordinances indicated a minimum lot size for this type of use was 8,000 square feet. These developers had proposed a lot size slightly smaller. This matter was debated among the board and various sectors of the white establishment community for the better part of a year. I don't know if I (originally) perceived it as a black/white issue. Incidentally, the developers were white. What I thought was attractive about the proposal was that this subdivision would likely attract young families to our community. At the time, I really didn't consider racial components at all. Those in opposition to the establishment of the subdivision said all manner of such things about how these homes would be flooded, etc. despite evidence to the contrary presented by this developer's engineer. The variance for lot size to permit the construction of this subdivision just barely was approved by the Board of Aldermen.

Despite all conflict and drama prior to the Board's decision to proceed with the project, it was an exciting thing to see Cedarstone subdivision get underway. As mayor, I was always pleased to see visible signs of progress throughout our town. Cedarstone was a 96-home subdivision, with the first 30 homes being built as part of phase 1. The other 66 homes were to be built in Phase 2. The average size home in part 1 was 1,200 square feet; the homes in phase 2 were around 1,500 square feet. This subdivision got underway around 2007, and even during the national financial crash of 2008, sales of homes in this subdivision continued. And the subdivision attracted mostly young families as well as a few empty nesters. In the end, Cedarstone was well received by the Town of Terry. Many of the fears of doom and gloom predicted by the naysayers simply never materialized.

The developer was well aware of the controversy and seemed to be most appreciative that I strongly advocated for the establishment of Cedarstone. In homage to my efforts to get this subdivision approved, the developers insisted on naming the main street in Part 1 of Cedarstone subdivision in my honor.

Description: Cedarstone Subdivision
Source: Central MS Planning & Development District; Jackson, MS

This was the first subdivision totally conceived and built out during my time as Mayor of Terry. Cedarstone was the first subdivision built in Terry with all underground utilities and sidewalks throughout. The main street in Part 1 (Nicholson Drive) is named in my honor.

Terry Park Subdivision

Terry Park Subdivision actually began in the late nineties under a previous administration. However, it seemed to languish with very little progress until after year 2000. In order to "jumpstart" the housing starts in Terry Park, it was decided that they would bring in several modular homes. The Town's zoning ordinances were poor to non-existent and included nothing to prohibit this action. In my opinion, not only were these homes not attractive, they negatively impacted the property values of the existing homes in this subdivision.

In the meantime, home builder Mr. Tommy Harkins, who eventually would go on to build our new City Hall, bought up the lion's share of the remaining available lots in Terry Park. These homes were attractive, they were a good value, and they seemed to sell very well.

Unfortunately, the nation-wide financial downturn in the economy had an indirect negative effect upon the Town of Terry as well. The developer of Terry Park subdivision eventually went bankrupt before the final street surface could be installed. Terry Park is located on 16th Section land, and it's a complicated matter to get the remaining lots built out, the final layer of asphalt surface put down, and the Town of Terry be in a position to accept future maintenance of this subdivision. Because of the poor condition of the streets and the vacant lots that need to be mowed, we got regular complaints from the residents of Terry Park subdivision regarding pot holes in the streets and rodents and snakes in the overgrown lots. This is quite understandable.

However at this point, the only options would be for the Town of Terry to lean on either the Hinds County Board of Supervisors and/or the Hinds County School District to pay the costs to overlay the streets in Terry Park subdivision. Of course, the town could just go ahead and fund the finish surface on the streets out of its general fund. (I'd like to reiterate that the developer is no longer in business). However, both the Hinds County Board of Supervisors and Hinds County Schools have been very good partners with the town. And they are likely financially strapped with a lot of other obligations as well. In the end, this matter is no longer my headache as I no longer serve as Mayor. This is a complicated issue with all kinds of political ramifications, and whatever solution is proposed, it's not likely to mutually satisfy the Board of Aldermen, the residents of Terry Park subdivision, the Hinds County School District, or the Hinds County Board of Supervisors.

Establishment of Sage Hill Subdivision

The Town of Terry had a choice of starter home community in either Cedarstone or Terry Park subdivisions. Those who wanted luxury homes with acreage could choose either Southfork Estates or Green Gable subdivisions. However, the town had no "move up" option for those seeking such.

In 2014, the same developer who had developed Cedarstone subdivision indicated that he had acquired a parcel of land further west along Morgan Drive and indicated that he would like to establish such a move-up or intermediate sized home subdivision. The developer indicated that he planned to work within the specifications of the town's subdivision and zoning ordinances and wouldn't need to apply for any type of variance. Essentially, his plan was to build fewer homes on larger lots to comply with the town's zoning and subdivision ordinances. The land was already zoned for what he was proposing, so there was no specific requirement to bring the matter to the Board of Aldermen. Similar to Cedarstone, Sage Hill subdivision is proposed to have all underground utilities. This subdivision got underway shortly after I left office in late 2015.

Description: The basic infrastructure of Sage Hill subdivision.
This is a planned "move-up" subdivision of about 25 homes
ranging in size from 1,500-1,600 sf. (November 2016)
Source: Rod Nicholson

Comprehensive Water Improvement Projects

When I first became Mayor in July 2005, about 25% of the residents were still on water wells or otherwise had not been connected to municipal water. Nearly 40% of the residents within the corporate limits were without municipal sewer and so had either a septic tank or a treatment plant. And the entire town was inundated and frustrated with the presence of a high level of organics in the water which gave it a color similar to weak tea.

One thing that I didn't realize until shortly after I took office was that the town's public utility (the Terry Water Service), was required to have an annual inspection by the Mississippi Department of Health. I remember the first annual inspection that I attended as Mayor. I was both surprised and embarrassed at how many violations that the town's water system was cited for.

A small amount of chlorine is typically added to disinfect most municipal water supplies. However, the water operator initially used a bit more in order to remove the color and reduce customer complaints. Eventually, the health department informed us that this practice of the addition of additional chlorine past a certain point often produces a higher than acceptable level of trihalomethane, a potential carcinogen, in our water samples. But, in order to minimize trihalomethanes in the water to be in compliance, we would get complaints from residents about the color in the water. Complaints included people having clothing (especially white or light colored clothing) that had essentially been destroyed after having been washed in this brown water. It was a circular problem to which there seemed to be no easy or simple solution.

We considered a number of alternatives to address this water quality issue and remain in compliance with the MDOH. Those alternatives included a form of reverse osmosis and purchase of water from other water systems.

- **Initial Plan to Purchase Water from City of Jackson, MS**

With the help of the Central MS Planning and Development District, the town was able to receive a small grant to consider the feasibility of purchasing water from the City of Jackson. Essentially, this proposed plan involved construction of an infrastructure system that would essentially provide a connection between Terry's water system and the City of Jackson that had an intake structure at the Sonny McDonald Industrial Park just north of town at Interstate Route 55 and Wynndale Road.

This certainly could have been a workable plan. However, the vast majority of the citizenry were adamantly opposed to considering this proposal. At the time, I thought what difference would it make where the water came from as long as we provided quality water in compliance with safety and standards established by the Mississippi Department of Health. However, I reluctantly acquiesced and backed away from this plan. However, in retrospect, I have to say that it may have been a good idea in the long run that we didn't give further consideration to this idea especially when you consider some of the significant water issues that the City of Jackson has had in recent years.

- **Development of a More Comprehensive Water Improvement Plan**

After the plan to purchase water through an interlocal agreement with the City of Jackson failed to materialize, we went back to the drawing board and considered a more comprehensive plan to not just address water quality issues, but water supply issues as well. This involved establishment of a new water well as well as providing access to as near to 100% of those residential and business water users within the corporate limits who were previously unserved. This included homes and businesses at both the far northern and far southern portions of town.

I was totally unprepared for and overwhelmed with all the administrative coordination and negotiations involved in acquiring a parcel of land for purposes of establishing a test well. The process costs about $20K each time a test well is dug, and even then there is no guarantee that the test well will yield either a suitable water supply and/or water quality. The town's consultant, Southern Consultants, Inc., was instrumental in doing an analysis that yielded some recommendations about where we were likely to find good water quality and sufficient water supply.

- **Challenges From Eastside Water Association**

Eastside Water Association had an existing water well less than a mile away. Unfortunately, some of the Town of Terry board members had strong ties to persons who operated the East Side Water Association. And sometimes, it appeared to me that these board members sympathized more with East Side Water Association than they did with the Board on which they were elected by the town to serve. Unfortunately, these types of conflicts are more commonplace in small towns in Mississippi than one might realize. In retrospect, either I as Mayor, the town attorney, or even the board members themselves should have recognized this obvious conflict of interest and been asked or forced to or voluntarily recuse themselves from casting votes on these particular matters.

People often act from what they feel and not necessarily from what they say. A LOT of the frustrations between whites and blacks has its roots in racially motivated transgressions from the past. There was a time in the past that apparently the whites who controlled Terry were selfish toward the black community. The blacks had petitioned the Town of Terry for water. It's my understanding that the whites in control at the time not just said "No", but "Hell No!" That's why organizations such as the Eastside Water Association came into existence. And although many of the whites associated with the Town of Terry who may have perpetuated these injustices are now gone, the charter members of the Eastside Water Association still remember how they were treated by "The Town". It was quite difficult for me to convince these people that although as Mayor I do represent the "The Town", I had nothing to do with whatever may have happened in the past. I'm just trying to do the best to ensure that the Town has a future.

Representatives from the Eastside Water Association and the Town of Terry met with the Mississippi Department of Environmental Quality to address East Side Water Association's concerns with the Town of Terry's proposal. In the end, the town received approval from MDEQ to establish the well at the location that we found high quality water.

Nonetheless, despite all the hardships and setbacks in establishing a new water well, the Lord blessed the town in our first try with a good source and good quality water. I cannot tell you how happy I was when I heard the news. I had our town engineering consultant, Mr. Jim Stewart, get a sample of the water from this new water source. I believe that to this day that this sample of water is in a Mason jar up at the City Hall building as a reminder of how far we had to come to achieve this goal of quality water for the town.

- **Providing Water to Unserved Areas**

As I indicated, the scope of the new water project was more comprehensive to include all unserved as well as underserved areas. This included a number of businesses along the east frontage road at the northern end of town as well as Terry Mission Church and other residential properties that had been recently annexed at the southern end of town.

Collis Hill – Sewer Service Problems

This is one area where decisions made by previous boards often became inadvertent problems for subsequent administrations. The Collis Hill community is a historically working class majority African American area within the Terry area. Until recently, the Collis Hill community was technically outside the Terry corporate limits. Even today, the vestiges of racism continue to be present throughout Mississippi, and the Collis Hill community is no exception.

I don't know all the past history of Collis Hill, and both black and whites for whatever reason seem to be reticent to openly discuss with me past racial issues and conflicts as they related to town matters. But rest assured that the racial tension continues to this day. By directive of the Mississippi Department of Health, every community in the state is within a prescribed water certificated area. However, these certificated areas don't always exactly align with the political jurisdictions. Although the Town of Terry operates its own water and sewer utility, the Collis Hill area's water certificate is under the East Side Water Association. However, the Town of Terry installs and maintains Collis Hill's sewer infrastructure. And therein is the root of the problem.

Almost from the beginning of my administration as Mayor, I have been aware of the fundamental hostility of the East Side Water Association toward the Town of Terry. After being in office for several months, it became apparent to me that the Collis Hill area was one of several major problems with the town's water/sewer utility. You see, a high percentage of persons in Collis Hill were not very timely in paying their $12/month fee for the town to maintain the sewer in this area. In many cases, we had persons who owed the town several thousand dollars and hadn't paid their sewer utility bill in years. We sent letters, made phone calls, and even threatened to shut down sewer service to seriously delinquent customers in those areas.

After we threatened to shut down the sewer service to the delinquent Collis Hill customers due to non-payment, we received a notice from the Mississippi Department of Environmental Quality (MDEQ) essentially stating that the Town of Terry was legally prohibited from shutting down the sewer service only as this could pose a health hazard to the resident. A potential health problem could arise if the water service (which was provided by Eastside Water Association) continued and the town shut down the sewer service.

MDEQ indicated that the town's only choices would be to shut the entire system (water and sewer service) down, or work out some type of payment plan with the delinquent customers and allow continuation of water and sewer services. Please note that I have previously indicated that the vast majority of the Collis Hill community receives water service from East Side Water Association. Thus, the Town of Terry has no control over those customers receiving their water service from East Side Water Association. And at the time when I was Mayor, most of the Collis Hill community was outside the political jurisdiction of the Town.

The Town of Terry then contacted the East Side Water association, explained our dilemma, and requested assistance in helping us to collect sewer maintenance fees from these delinquent customers. We even expressed a willingness to compensate the East Side Water Association for their efforts in assisting the town. I can only assume because of historically negative relationship between East Side Water Association and the Town of Terry, East Side Water Association was none too cooperative. I don't know all the history of the many rural water associations in Mississippi. But it's quite possible that a large number of these rural water associations may have come into existence because many municipalities either wouldn't or couldn't extend sewer service into these largely poor, African American communities.

A number of these delinquent customers were aware of the town's dilemma and often taunted the town that they were aware of their delinquency and refused to honor their sewer maintenance obligations. I must say that there were some who did make an effort to become current on their bills. However, seriously delinquent sewer bills from the Collis

Hill community were a significant problem for the town during my time that I served as Mayor.

One prominent citizen within the Collis Hill community even told the Board that she didn't pay because she and her family had been "promised by a previous administration that they would never have to pay anything to the town" for her sewer service. We asked her to produce documents stating such and/or provide the town with a name(s) of person(s) from previous board administrations who may have told her this. However, this never came to pass.

I cannot tell you how many hours that we spent having our town attorney work on a legal solution to this issue. Our attorney did indicate that this was going to be an uphill battle to forcibly collect on the delinquent customers in the Collis Hill community because Collis Hill was outside of the Town of Terry's corporate limits. As Mayor, I felt like the town was between a rock and a hard place. On the one hand, state statute prohibits municipalities from subsidizing one town activity from a pot of money from another. In other words, the water utility was supposed to be totally self sustaining. Of course, I didn't want to incur the political backlash by raising the water/sewer utility rates on the entire town to essentially subsidize those who refused to pay. In order to reduce the financial hemorrhage of sewer costs to maintain the sewer system in Collis Hill, the board did eventually agree to increase the sewer rates to $17/month for Collis Hill residents only. The others who received water and sewer service through the Town of Terry had sewer rates based on a formula based on a percentage of their actual monthly water usage.

Previous administrations had avoided directly addressing this issue. However, I was determined to move the town forward. And I began to realize that the town cannot move forward unless historical issues such as these that have held the town back be addressed.

Collis Hill was one of several areas that were submitted to the Courts for annexation in 2013. In late 2014, Collis Hill was approved by the Courts for annexation into the Town of Terry. However, shortly before I left office, the annexation was contested. So, ultimately I don't know whether this issue will be addressed or resolved to the satisfaction of the town.

Construction of the New Ella Bess Austin Municipal Library

When I moved to Terry in 1999, the town's library was a single-wide well worn trailer located on Cunningham Avenue in the southwest corner of the Village Square Park. The library was so small, and there was a makeshift drive-through for people to pick up books. Initially, it was open only a few days per week, and even then, it was open for a few hours on those days. Before this trailer had been converted to the town's library, it had been a video store.

Description: Old Terry Municipal Library (Front)
Source: Central MS Planning & Development District; Jackson, MS

Description: Old Terry Municipal Library (Rear)
Source: Central MS Planning & Development District; Jackson, MS

When I first became Mayor, this trailer-library was open only a few days per week, and even then only a few hours on these days. In this trailer-library, there was hardly enough room to do anything except pick up and check out books.

Several hundred yards west of the trailer library, Copiah Bank had established a branch office in another trailer just west along Cunningham Avenue as well. Unfortunately, a rare bank robbery event occurred at the Terry branch. In addition, I don't believe that this branch yielded the business traffic that this bank's board of directors had hoped. So, the bank's board of directors apparently decided to close the Terry branch of the Copiah Bank. Initially, I was disappointed and contacted the Copiah Bank management to encourage them to remain open for a few months longer. However, the bank's board of directors indicated that they were firm in their decision to close the Terry branch.

After the construction of the City Hall building, I had given a lot of thought to my vision of what our main street (Cunningham Avenue) would look like. I had lamented our pitiful trailer-library (which incidentally, was located directly across the street from our newly constructed City Hall building) for a while, and I thought that it might be nice to have a more traditional brick and mortar municipal library building on Cunningham

Avenue. Because this property is 16th Section land, I contacted Hinds County School Board, explained my proposal for this old Copiah Bank property, and asked that they give the Town of Terry first right of refusal to develop the land. The School Board got back with me and indicated that they had no objection to this use.

I then asked the Board of Aldermen to authorize me to begin the slow, painstaking task of finding grant funding for a new library building. I took what I had learned from the construction of our City Hall building to assist me in this undertaking. I had been so pleased working with the architect from the City Hall building that I called on him again to assist the town in this effort. This time, though, he was more hesitant to accept a flat fee for his services (as I previously indicated, many architects here in Mississippi prefer the cost-plus method in municipal infrastructure projects). However, my counter-proposal/rationale to him was that after the project is completed, his work would be prominently displayed on our main street forever. And that kind of advertisement is priceless. I don't know if it convinced him or not, but we did finally agree to terms and conditions for a flat fee to design the Terry municipal library.

Although we were quite pleased with the City Hall building overall, my regrets were that the bathrooms were a bit too large and the board meeting room was a bit too small. Now although building costs tend to increase with the size of the building, I was very cognizant not to construct the library building too small. Even if it meant that it might take a bit longer to secure additional funds needed to construct a larger building. A larger building would better accommodate anticipated growth and community demand for library services.

After several revisions of the draft plan, it was decided that the library building would be a minimum of 4,000 square feet and would include a small kitchen, both a kids and an adult section each with its own large book/intake reference desk, six computer stations, a separate office for the head librarian, and one private meeting room. We also looked at the library's current book inventory and added a percentage in sizing the book shelf space to accommodate anticipated growth and usage of this library. Of course, we included off-street parking in front of the library (primarily for patrons) and back parking (for employees). Parking along Cunningham

Avenue (where the library would be located) is prohibited to minimize traffic congestion.

Perhaps I am prejudiced, but I really liked this architect's plans. Even though we are a small town forever on a limited budget, his plans always seem to maximize use of space. His use of high ceilings added volume to the interior space as well as maintain physical comfort especially during the extended summer months.

In order to get the community excited about the next infrastructure project, we worked with our architect to also produce a rendering of our new library and had it prominently displayed in our new City Hall building. This did wonders for the morale of the library patrons (who often visited City Hall on other business), the town staff, and the general public. A place that had almost stagnated for thirty years was now seeing a few positive changes.

- **Friction From the Board Regarding Municipal Library**

As excited as I and many of the community were in anticipation of the new library building, a couple of the board members weren't as pleased. The usual type of delay tactics were employed by various board members similar to what happened during the construction of the city hall building. It was just that the same games being played by different board members. The counter-proposal that came to me from one of the board members was to consider building the library on land owned by some of the African American local political establishment as well as a relative of this board member.

In addition to the obvious conflict of interest between this board member and land owner, this land was also in a flood prone area. Technically, construction of a building could be permitted but would require significant amounts of fill dirt to ensure that the building slab was above the base flood elevation. This could have added more than $50K to the cost of the building. Funding was difficult enough without unnecessarily adding to the costs out the gate.

In the end, the board stayed with the original plan to build along Cunningham Avenue at the site of the old Copiah Bank. An advantage of this was that the existing trailer-library could remain open and continue to provide library services to the community while the new library building was being constructed.

- **Unexpected Benefit Gained During Municipal Library Construction**

As previously indicated, the original library construction plans included a separate room to hold the HVAC equipment. However, during the construction of the library building, the contractor pointed out that the roof pitch was steep enough to place the HVAC equipment in the attic area provided we use sufficient bracing during construction to properly support the equipment. Placing the equipment in the attic area above allowed us to use this space as a second meeting room which was essentially the same size as the other meeting room in the original plans. So, instead of one meeting room, the new library contains two meeting rooms essentially the same size.

I along with many of the town's residents was excited to see the new library come together. The library building Open House had a standing room only crowd with people from the town, Hinds County and beyond in attendance. We even had one of the Deputy Secretaries from the Housing and Urban Development (HUD) from Washington, DC to come to the library open house. The administrators from the Jackson-Hinds Library system were also on hand and were most pleased to be a part of an event that seemed to have taken forever to come to fruition.

Description: Ella Bess Austin – Terry Municipal Public Library
Source: Central MS Planning & Development District; Jackson, MS

This replaced the old single-wide trailer library. The new library was more than 4,000 square feet; had separate children's and adult sections, and two private meeting rooms for tutoring and other community services.

Rehabilitation of Cunningham Avenue

As a member of the Metropolitan Planning Organization (MPO), I lobbied for the town to receive funds to rehabilitate our streets, many of which had not received any type of maintenance for almost 30 years. The funds that we used to rehabilitate Cunningham Avenue were originally intended for our major north-south street (Utica Street). However, our town engineer indicated that there were so many design deviations and deficiencies along Utica Street that would require correction prior to overlay, it was decided that completing a project on Cunningham Avenue would be better than losing the rehabilitation funds altogether.

- **Continuous Sidewalks Installed on Both Sides of Cunningham Avenue**

  Along Cunningham Avenue, one requirement from the Federal Highway Administration (FHWA) was that the town install a sidewalk the entire street length on at least one side of the street. There was existing sidewalk along various sections of both sides of Cunningham Avenue. However, the sidewalk was not continuous on either side. The FHWA was very gracious in working with us. The town was granted a design deviation that essentially allowed us to put in a 36" sidewalk on both sides (in lieu of the standard 42" sidewalk) to meet existing width sidewalk areas. This was all bid within budget, and the work was completed significantly ahead of schedule. I don't recall getting a lot of pushback from the Board as this was much of the town's matching funds were covered by the ARRA funds (Economic Stimulus funds provided to a number of communities post-Hurricane Katrina). Having sidewalks encouraged people to get out and exercise more. A number of people began using the sidewalks to walk to school, walking to our downtown area, visiting the bank, going to the post office, Village Square Park and eventually our new Fred's Super Store which were all located along Cunningham Avenue.

Improvements in the Town of Terry's Fire Insurance Rating

Each municipality in Mississippi is rated on a scale of 1 to 10, with 1 being the best and 10 being the worst, for fire insurance purposes. Municipalities generally have an option of extending their fire insurance rating into adjacent unincorporated areas particularly if it is to that unincorporated area's benefit to have the municipal insurance rating assigned to it. If the insurance rating is assigned to an unincorporated area, this must also be approved by the Mississippi Insurance Rating Bureau.

When I became Mayor back in 2005, the Town of Terry had an insurance rating of 9. This rating had been unchanged since 1962. As Mayor, I certainly wanted to improve the town's insurance rating. A more attractive insurance rating is one of several factors that potential businesses take into consideration when making a decision to locate in a particular area. When a business decides to establish a presence in a town, that business typically will invest from $3 - $5 million into facilities, and understandably they want some reasonable assurance that should some type of unfortunate incident occur that could threaten their business that the municipality is capable of providing timely support and fire protection. It's only good business when you think about it.

When I initially approached the Terry Volunteer Fire Department to see what could be done to improve the town's fire insurance rating, I didn't get much encouragement or support. The collective response from the TVFD was that efforts to improve the town's rating would essentially be a waste of time. I remember asking the question whether an attempt had ever been made to improve the town's insurance rating and/or what obstacles would we have to overcome to make this happen. The response was that it couldn't be done and that it was a waste of time. I truly could not understand why anyone in public service would not want to at least make an effort to improve any condition that could be of benefit to everyone.

Because of the lack of support from the Terry volunteer fire department, I went directly to the Mississippi Insurance Rating Bureau, explained where the town currently was with its insurance rating, and asked what the criteria was to be considered for a reduction (improvement) in the town's insurance rating. According to the Insurance Rating Bureau, there were a number of factors which must be taken into consideration. And these included overall water capacity, a certified minimum number of operable water hydrants fairly evenly distributed throughout the community, and a certified minimum water pressure from the majority of these hydrants. Because the Town of Terry is relatively small with much of the population concentrated in a certain area, having a centrally located fire station would be an asset in the consideration for improvement in the town's fire insurance rating.

This is an issue that I worked on intermittently over several years. I began to reconsider the possibility again shortly after we completed our comprehensive water project. With the establishment a new water well system, I knew that we could meet the water capacity criteria. Also as part of the comprehensive water improvement project, we repaired, replaced, and/or installed a number of hydrants throughout town. So I felt that we could demonstrate to the state rating insurance bureau that we had an operable system in place worthy of a reduction (improvement) in the town's fire insurance rating.

However, in order that we demonstrate that the town had met all criteria for an insurance rating reduction, we needed to conduct a flow test on the town's water system and provide those results to the Mississippi Insurance Rating Bureau for their approval. I contacted the Terry Volunteer Fire Department, explained the situation and inquired when they could complete a flow test on our water system. The Terry Volunteer Fire Department indicated that it wasn't the volunteer fire department's job to conduct the flow test. According to the VFD, conducting the flow test was the responsibility of the town's Public Works Department. When I approached the Public Works department, they indicated that it was the responsibility of the Terry Volunteer Fire Department.

After this matter going back and forth for several months, a gentleman from the MS Insurance Rating Bureau apparently had sympathy on the town's dilemma. Apparently, this gentleman had knowledge of how to conduct a flow test. However, on the day that the flow test was to be conducted by the insurance rating bureau, we did have personnel from both the volunteer fire department and public works departments present to assist this gentleman from the State of Mississippi Rating Insurance Bureau.

After the flow test was completed, the insurance rating guy indicated that the Town of Terry had made sufficient improvements in its water infrastructure system to warrant an improvement from a "9" to an "8". The Town of Terry received its notification from the MS Insurance Rating Bureau in mid-2011, that our fire insurance rating had been improved. This represented the first improvement of the town's fire insurance rating in almost 50 years.

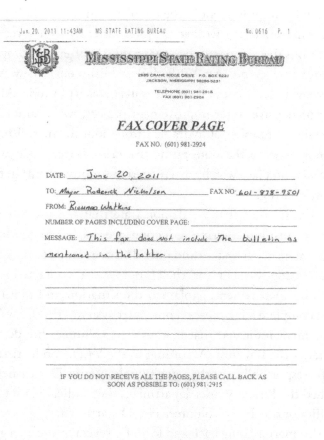

Jun. 20. 2011 11:43AM   MS STATE RATING BUREAU   No. 0616   P. 1

MISSISSIPPI STATE RATING BUREAU

2985 CRANE RIDGE DRIVE   P.O. BOX 5231
JACKSON, MISSISSIPPI 39296-5231

TELEPHONE (601) 981-2915
FAX (601) 981-2924

FAX COVER PAGE

FAX NO. (601) 981-2924

DATE: _June 20, 2011_

TO: _Mayor Roderick Nicholson_ ___ FAX NO: _601-878-9501_

FROM: _Richard Watkins_

NUMBER OF PAGES INCLUDING COVER PAGE: ___

MESSAGE: _This fax does not include The bulletin as mentioned in the letter._

IF YOU DO NOT RECEIVE ALL THE PAGES, PLEASE CALL BACK AS
SOON AS POSSIBLE TO: (601) 981-2915

MISSISSIPPI STATE RATING BUREAU

2685 CRANE RIDGE DRIVE   P.O. BOX 5231
JACKSON, MISSISSIPPI 39296-5231

TELEPHONE (601) 981-2915
FAX (601) 981-2924

June 21, 2011

The Honorable Roderick Nicholson
Mayor of Terry
Post Office Box 327
Terry, Mississippi 39170-0327

Dear Mayor Nicholson:

PUBLIC FIRE PROTECTION FACILITIES
TOWN OF TERRY
HINDS COUNTY, MISSISSIPPI

Reference is made to the recent survey and grading of Terry's fire prevention and fire protection facilities. The purpose of this survey was to gather information needed to determine a fire insurance classification which may be used to develop fire insurance rates. We are pleased to advise the fire defenses of Terry have advanced, and an improved fire insurance classification of Eighth Class has been confirmed effective June 15, 2011.

Although the town now grades Class Eight for fire insurance purposes, we would like to make the following improvement statements in order to safely maintain this classification.

1. Strengthen the water distribution system so that 2000 gallons per minute with a residual pressure of twenty (20) pounds would be available in commercial areas and 1000 gallons per minute with a residual pressure of twenty (20) pounds would be available in residential areas. We would suggest this be done under advice of a competent engineer.

2. Provide auxiliary engines such as gasoline, diesel, butane or natural gas powered, on enough well pumps, so that you could maintain a pumping capacity of at least equal to the maximum daily water consumption rate. These engines should be stationary at the wells. This would be very critical in the event of failure of normal electric power supply.

3. Maintain an annual inspection and operation program of all gate valves in the water distribution system. This would ensure that all could be found and that they are open. All valves should be located and numbered and legible records kept of all inspections and repairs.

4. Increase the number of volunteers responding to all structure fires so that an average of eight (8) to ten (10) volunteers would respond to each call per fire department pumper

The Honorable Roderick Nicholson   - 2 -   June 21, 2011
Mayor of Terry

5. Continue to maintain a training program for all firefighters. A minimum program of training
    would consist of monthly drills of two (2) hour duration supplemented by a local school held
    by an outside instructor. Training would consist of actual evolutions rather than just talk
    sessions and records should be kept of all training sessions. Each of the volunteers should
    complete the State Volunteer Certification Course.

6. Update and provide for the strict enforcement of a modern Building Code, Gas Code,
    Electric Code and Fire Prevention Code. Enforcement of these Codes would be provided
    through the receipt of applications, issuing of permits and inspections by a competent
    inspector. Records of these operations would include filing of the forms and notes of the
    inspector as he makes inspections with any follow-up enforcement needed.

These improvement statements refer only to the fire insurance rating classification of your town. Our
comments are not for property loss prevention or life safety purposes and no life safety or property
loss prevention recommendations are made.

As you may know, the public fire protection insurance classification number is used as only one of
several elements in developing some individual property insurance rates. Individual property fire
rates are also dependent upon specific construction, occupancy, private protection and exposure from
adjacent buildings.

We are pleased to attach a bulletin that is being distributed which outlines the procedure to be
followed in changing fire insurance rates on properties in Terry based on the new classification.

Your interest in fire protection and prevention is commended, and we will be happy to be of
assistance should you call upon us.

Yours very truly,

Richard Watkins
Field Rating Representative
Public Protection

jb

CC: Fire Chief Eddie Chambless
      Terry Fire Department
      Post Office Box 402
      Terry, Mississippi 39170-0402

Description: Document Approving the Reduction (Improvement) in the Town's Fire Insurance Rating. This is the first improvement in insurance rating in the Town in almost 50 years!
Source: State of Mississippi Insurance Rating Bureau; Jackson, MS

Description: Fire Station – Public Works Building
Source: Central MS Planning & Development District; Jackson, MS

This structure was at the site of and replaced the old City Hall building

Construction of Combination Terry Public Works/Fire Station

In 2008, the Town of Terry City Hall was relocated into the newly constructed building on Cunningham Avenue. The Public Works Department remained in the original City Hall on Railroad Avenue. I think it's kind of ironic that our Public Works Department in many ways is the heart and soul that keeps things going with the town. Yet, they were located in the most pitiful, dilapidated building. Being Mayor in a small town with a very limited budget and tax base was an issue almost every day.

However, the building that housed the Public Works Department was deteriorating rapidly, and something needed to be done before the building was to literally fall down before our eyes. I discussed this matter with building designer Mr. Uriel Pineda. I had also previously shared with him our success with improving the town's insurance rating and how I had hoped to improve the town's insurance rating even further with a centrally located fire station eventually.

It was during one of these conversations that we kind of wondered out loud whether the location of the old City Hall building property could re-purposed to construct both a fire station and a public works building as well. Mr. Pineda indicated that because of similar uses, he felt that these functions could possibly be combined under one roof.

The location for this building would be perfect for both municipal functions. First of all, this was the only parcel of land owned outright by the town. Secondly, for purposes of a fire station, this location was fairly centrally located and was within 5 miles of all the existing corporate limits and proposed areas for annexation. Locating a fire station can be very tricky and politically controversial. Everyone can generally agree that the presence of a fire station in town is vital. However, the location of the fire station can generate substantial disagreement amongst the townsfolk.

This proposed fire station/public works building location was right across from the railroad tracks which in and of itself generated a degree of daily intermittent noise. Any noise generated by a proposed fire station at this location would be no greater than the intermittent noise already generated by train traffic coming through town each day.

We then contacted the MS Emergency Management Agency to determine whether the town could accomplish this combination fire station – public works building under one roof as had been originally suggested. MEMA had more concern with the construction of the fire station portion than with the public works portion because at the time the town received insurance rebate funds from the State of Mississippi to support the functions of the Terry Volunteer Fire Department. MEMA indicated that having both functions under one roof was acceptable provided that there is "complete internal positive separation" between the two functions in this proposed building. Essentially, this means that a continuous wall between the two functions must exist similar to how residential townhomes are constructed. The only allowed access between the two buildings must be through an external rather than an internal door.

With the conditional approval of the design concept from the MS Emergency Management Agency, the matter was brought to the board for their consideration and approval. Shortly thereafter, we had the property surveyed to ensure there was sufficient real estate available to accomplish our intended goal. The survey information was then forwarded to our building designer to superimpose on various plans that he had begun working on. Although the our plans were ambitious and the available land was a bit tight, we decided that there was enough real estate to accomplish our goals for the proposed combination fire station-public works building. The next task was to seek funding from outside sources to make this a reality. Although there was elation from the community about the possibility of construction of another much needed municipal infrastructure project, there were some concerns of the board and volunteer fire department. Again.

- **Terry Volunteer Fire Department**

I sincerely tried to get along with these guys from the Terry Volunteer fire department. But one has to understand that getting along is a two-way street. One thing that was evident to me that the racial makeup of the volunteer fire department was about over 90% white in a community with a roughly 50/50 ratio of black and white residents. The racial composition of the volunteer fire department did not seem even remotely reflective of the community. However, I could never be sure exactly what went on in the Terry Volunteer Fire Department because they absolutely refused to provide me with records of their training, who their members were, their activities, etc. I did not think that this was an overreach on my part to expect this information as Mayor of the town in which the Terry Volunteer Fire Department provided services.

For years, I had been trying to get the State of MS Rating Bureau to improve the town's fire insurance rating and needed this information for the Rating Bureau's evaluation. The Terry Volunteer Fire Department refused to provide me anything toward this effort. Certain members of Terry VFD were especially critical of and outspoken against my efforts to effect any improvements to the Town of Terry's fire insurance rating or the VFD.

On more than one occasion, the white Terry VFD members told me personally that I was wasting my time in building a new centrally located fire department and/or trying to improve the town's fire insurance rating. They became even more incensed when we eventually got both done not because of Terry VFD's assistance, but in spite of the Terry Volunteer Fire Department's efforts to be an obstruction to these things becoming a reality. To this day, I really don't know why. But if I had to speculate it was that most of the leaders within the VFD were staunch racists didn't want to see a progressive African American leader. The volunteer fire department was not interested in achieving any progress in our community and certainly not under the leadership of a African American Mayor. Even today, this mentality continues to be reflective of far too many in the State of Mississippi.

- **More Friction From the Board Regarding Fire Station/Public Works Project**

As excited as I and many in the community were about this project, there were concerns voiced from some of the Board members. In addition, a lot of the pressure/responsibility (and perhaps rightly so) was put on me as the Mayor to seek sources of funding and coordinate a temporary move of the public works department while continuing public works department services to the public. In addition, because this project involved both the demolition of a building and the establishment of another building, an environmental document with findings had to be completed and paid for. And this board was not supportive of using any general funds for this project despite the apparent and dire need.

By this time, I was neither surprised nor deterred by the almost constant funk regarding any proposed municipal infrastructure improvements from this board. It really didn't occur to me until shortly before I began writing these memoirs that their motivation was really just to thwart progress because these things were being accomplished under my leadership as Mayor. If it wasn't one of them, it was the other putting up such a public fuss and complaint about anything. They suggested that we consider another location. When I asked what other locations that we as a Board might consider, they could never suggest even one.

I had tried to seek grant funding, but most sources either we couldn't demonstrate enough need for this particular type of project (many of these projects we were competing with communities in the Mississippi Delta whose demographics demonstrated far greater need). The only optimistic source was a low interest loan through US Department of Agriculture.

I clearly remember one board meeting, and one of the items on the agenda was to pursue funding from some source that I was cautiously optimistic of it being successful. The board had been notified of the expectation to make a decision as I had a limited window of time to prepare and submit a grant application. Despite having discussed this matter intermittently for more than a year, one of the board members indicated that she felt the process was moving too fast and that we needed to slow down our pursuit of this project. Another board member who had been absent when the meeting began but shortly before we were to take a vote on the matter that they appeared with their "concerns." In my opinion, these were nothing but delay tactics by these certain board members.

At this point, I'd also like to mention that we had a white attorney named Kurt Guthrie who normally attended most board meetings and was usually silent during these discussions. However, this time, the attorney, visibly irritated by this board's collective antics, interjected himself into the discussion. Mr. Guthrie asked this board member who appeared just before the vote was to be taken what specific concerns did they have that would prevent the Mayor from proceeding with a grant application for this project. After all, we had informally discussed this matter for months prior to this. As adamant as this board member had been five minutes prior all of a sudden they had no concerns. Mr. Guthrie then asked the other board member also in opposition did she still have any concerns that would require a delay in further consideration of this matter. Both board members meekly said they had none.

There was a reason that I mentioned previously that the attorney was white. As a transplant from the Midwest, I had never witnessed black people be so openly subservient to white people simply because they are white and how often African Americans are often so antagonistic with other African Americans until I came to Mississippi. I'm not necessarily saying that all Southern Blacks are this way, but I have witnessed more than my share that are. And I think this matter clearly illustrates just that. If it weren't for this white attorney, these African American aldermen would have never voted for the fire station/public works building (sadly) because I look like them.

• MS Archives and History Concerns in Demolition of Old City Hall

Fortunately, the town was able to secure a combination of grant and loan funding to complete this project. In addition, the town was able to include the cost of funding the environmental documents required as part of the allowable costs in the grant portion. The town contracted through the Central MS Planning and Development District in order to complete this Environmental Assessment Report (EAR) and Finding of No Significant Impacts (FONSI).

One day, I received a call from the Planning District stating that they would be unable to complete the FONSI. Essentially, the issue was that the MS Department of Archives and History would not give a sign off to allow removal of the old City Hall building. According to the Planning District, the old City Hall building was of significant historical importance to the community and that MS Archives and History could not grant their approval to demolish this building. This is the same dilapidated City Hall building that I inherited when I first became Mayor in 2005. It is absolutely amazing that this building did not simply fall in because its condition was so poor. This is a building that should have been condemned. In addition, the building was not in its original state because it had a poorly constructed addition that also was in a rapidly deteriorating state.

According to the CMPDD, the issue with MS Archives and History was the only unresolved issue that stood in the way of them providing a Finding of No Significant Impact and thus completing all required environmental considerations to permit the project to move forward.

As a Civil Engineer with both an environmental background as well as experience in working on environmental matters with state and federal government, I contacted the MS Department of Archives and History directly regarding this matter. In the end, we were able to work with the MS Archives and History and mitigate and address the concerns that they had to permit this state agency giving their signoff approval to be included with the FONSI.

• MEMA Denial of the Use of Fire Funds To Complete the Project

One final frustrating issue that happened was that the MS Emergency Management Agency indicated to the Town of Terry that we would be unable to use any fire insurance rebate funds to construct the fire station portion of the project. Construction of an in-town fire station was an original goal of the previous Mayor Billy Pechloff. I just bought in to Mayor Pechloff's vision for an in town fire station and continued to pursue it under my administration. I found it both disappointing and amazing that just as we were on the verge of actually constructing this project that MEMA would prohibit the town from so doing. Under his administration, former Mayor Pechloff had established an account where the fire insurance rebate funds were essentially banked with the purpose of eventually constructing the fire station. Annual reports filed with the state essentially stating this purpose year after year. In the end, we had to both do value engineering to cut construction costs as well as increase the amount of loan to fund this project without the fire insurance rebate funds.

Once the fire station was completed, the goal was to apply seek grant funding to purchase brand new fire trucks for the 2-bay facility. After this, the plan was for the town to go back to the MS Rating Bureau to petition for a further reduction (improvement) in the town's insurance rating. Because of all the conflict that I began to have with the board shortly after my re-election in 2013, I was unable to pursue neither the acquisition of fire trucks nor a further reduction in the town's fire insurance rating.

- **Claims that Fire Station Bays Were Constructed Too Small**

I'd like to bring up another point that in my opinion demonstrates the hateful, racist nature of the Terry Volunteer Fire Department and the publisher of the now defunct Terry News newspaper toward me. Somehow these entities got in their respective minds that the reason that the town didn't immediately purchase fire trucks was because the bays had been constructed too small to accommodate a standard sized fire truck. The fire department and the local newspaper then brought this information to the board.

And just because these (white) people told that to them, I guess that it must have been true.

One day, I had a passing conversation with the town's Public Works Director. Apparently, the town had received a sales visit from a fire truck vendor and had informed us that the City of Crystal Springs, our neighboring town to the south, would be taking possession of a new fire truck. I then called this sales person who informed me that the size of fire truck was the same exact size and had the same specifications as what he would recommend for the town should we decide to do business with him.

On the day that the fire truck was to be delivered to the City of Crystal Springs, we arranged for the sales person to alter his trip route to stop through the Town of Terry. We had the driver to actually park the fire truck in the Terry Fire Department bay and take a picture to verify to both the Terry News, the VFD, and to this doubting board of aldermen that the dimensions of the bays were suitable for a standard sized fire truck. In the end, we had more than enough room. And this truck was also equipped with a ladder (although that wasn't a specific fire fighting requirement in our community). Of course, I never received nor expected any type of acknowledgement or apology from the Terry News, the Terry Volunteer Fire Department, or any of the board members.

Description: Fire Truck Parked In Terry Fire Station Bay
Source: Rod Nicholson, Mayor

The Board of Aldermen, the Terry Volunteer Fire Department, and the *Terry News* somehow got the impression that the reason that we didn't have a fire truck was because the truck bays of new building had been sized too small to fit standard sized trucks. This picture clearly dispels this notion.

Fred's Inc. Super Dollar Store Comes to Terry

As a part-time small town Mayor, one has to wear a lot of hats in order to keep things going and certainly to get anything of significance accomplished. For every success that may be apparent, there may have been nine other failures that most people are never aware of. As I have stated on a number of occasions, the "efforts" take up as much time as the "successes". It's just that with the "efforts", you don't have as much to show that you tried.

The Town of Terry doesn't have any kind of Chamber of Commerce or Department of Economic Development. Still as a small town, part-time Mayor, the constituents expect me to be a part of the Rotary Club, periodically lobby and meet with members of the legislature, and demonstrate some tangible means of progress and success on behalf of the town. I have to meet with people, have breakfast, have lunch, have dinner, meet with people the weekends (sometime even on Sundays), etc. And I didn't really mind it (most of the time) because I understood and accepted that this could be a part of this when I signed up for the job. Because there was no economic development office, by default in many cases the Mayor has to serve in this capacity. Despite the fact that I do not necessarily have a business or marketing background to represent the town. Well, I just had to learn along the way.

Shortly after the fire station/public works project got underway, I received a call that some business person wanted to meet at City Hall. Actually, it was a young guy who indicated that he was representing the interests of a business development client. Although I did agree to meet with this gentleman at City Hall, he declined to give me the specifics of what economic development client he was representing. He did, however, indicate that his client was a national retail business and that he would like for me to show him various available parcels that his client might be interested in. Of course, as Mayor, I was curious and asked at least a couple of other times, but he politely declined each time. Now, this was a first for this Mayor! However, he did eventually reveal to me who he represented. However, he strongly suggested that I keep our meeting confidential. Business people often desire confidentiality in matters where land acquisition is required. It's amazing how valuable a piece of swamp land can become if its owner gets the impression that the potential buyer has deep pockets. So I did understand his position.

The parcel that Fred's Superstore wanted was on 16th Section land. This type of land can be particularly tricky, problematic, and bureaucratic to come to mutual terms. First of all, it can only be leased. Secondly, all leases have to include an escalation clause to account for inflation. Thirdly, 16th Section land leases have to be coordinated and approved through the local school board, the county commission or supervisors, and the Secretary of State's office in Mississippi. In the Town of Terry, most of our main street (Cunningham Avenue) is 16th Section land.

Apparently, this retail representative had done his homework. Early in the process, they indicated that they would prefer to work with me directly as much as possible because the town had a board that had a reputation of being difficult to work with. I told them that at some point, the matter had to be brought to the board because the Mayor is simply unable to independently approve decisions such as these.

At any rate, we worked through things. Out of respect to the board, I did write a personal note to the board several days before the matter to approve this project was to be formally presented for their consideration, approval, and confidentiality until the board meeting. And of course, during the board meeting, a couple of the board members whined about their concerns about exterior colors and such but ultimately the measure passed. The proposed building would be approximately 16,000 square feet of retail space that would sell food items, clothing, cleaning supplies, and small appliances. In addition, a full-service pharmacy was planned to be included. This was truly a godsend considering the town's only locally owned pharmacy had closed its doors only a few months earlier. To some people, this may seem small, but it was significant to a town with a limited tax base that economically had been stagnant for years. When Fred's Superstore opened in late September 2013, it was very well received by the Terry community.

Description: Fred's Super Store; Terry, MS.
Source: Central MS Planning & Development District; Jackson, MS

This 16,000 square foot retail store included a full-service pharmacy, clothing items, appliances, and non-perishable grocery items. Fred's does in excess of $2 million annually.

Congressional Funds Received for Road Improvements for Hinds County Small Towns

Shortly after I was elected as Mayor in 2005, the Town of Terry was one of four towns in Hinds County earmarked by Congressman Bennie Thompson (D-MS) to receive $250,000 funding for road improvements. The other towns in Hinds County selected to receive funding were Bolton, Edwards, and Utica, MS. I was a very newly elected Mayor and so a lot of the nuances about how things are done I had not yet become familiar with. However, one thing that I thought was most unusual was that the grant was to be administered through Hinds County, not the Town of Terry. There was a formal announcement that our town would be receiving these funds. There was certainly a demonstrated need for the road improvements in town, and I was eager to see some of our much needed streets be paved. Despite my calls and letters to both Congressman Thompson's office and to the Hinds County Board of Supervisors, it seemed like little to no progress was being made. Because the grant was administered through the Hinds County Board of Supervisors and the MS Department of Transportation, the Town of Terry had no control over the selection of the consultant, the bidding procedures, or the timetable to design, bidding and/or actual completion of the project.

It took five years of calls, complaints and letters to all these offices before any physical progress was made. I decided from here on out that as Mayor, I would not accept a grant that the town did not have the ability to administer. This project was not completed until late 2010.

Brick Mailbox Controversy
in Southfork Estates subdivision

As part of the Congressional earmark of funds to pave roads in Terry, the Board of Aldermen did agree that the tentative list of streets to be paved to include Morgan Drive and both streets in the Southfork Estates subdivision (Levon Owens Drive and West Levon Owens Drive). However, the Town was informed by the Hinds County's engineer that all brick mailboxes in Southfork Estates subdivision had to be moved prior to road paving.

In my opinion, the problem with the roads in Southfork Estates subdivision especially lie with the previous administration that prematurely accepted the infrastructure from the developer without certification that the roads had been properly constructed. And once the roads had been accepted, the town had no legal recourse to compel the developer to meet his obligations to correct these deficiencies. In addition to a substandard road surface, the Town of Terry accepted responsibility of Southfork Estates subdivision without requiring the developer to provide sewer, natural gas, or properly file enforceable subdivision covenants.

One of the residents of Southfork had recently constructed his new home and brick mailbox as was the custom in this subdivision. Understandably, he was none too pleased with having to remove his mailbox, but the roads in this upscale subdivision of acreage properties were in deplorable condition. The majority of persons in Southfork were also disappointed at being told that the removal of brick mailboxes were a requirement before funds could be spent to rehabilitate the roads. However, the overwhelming majority of the Southfork residents also agreed to remove their brick mailboxes at their expense per the directive of the Hinds County Engineer.

However, this new resident and his wife brought the matter to the Terry Board of Aldermen. In the end, this couple were the only residents in Southfork

Estates subdivision who were financially compensated solely on the basis of personal preference for the removal of their brick mailbox. What makes this even more remarkable is that this person was also on the town's Board of Aldermen. And the Board of Aldermen didn't hesitate to approve this action.

Despite these questionable actions of blatant preferential treatment, this was a much needed project. Paving the roads in Southfork made significant improvements in the appearance and was well received and appreciated by its residents.

Description: Southfork Estates subdivision; Terry, MS.
Source: Central MS Planning & Development District; Jackson, MS

In my 10+ years as Mayor, the Town of Terry paved the streets, installed natural gas utility, and extended municipal sewer into the Southfork Estates subdivision. Retrofitting this subdivision with infrastructure was a very expensive and cumbersome undertaking because the homes are spaced fairly far apart (lot sizes in this luxury home subdivision are a minimum of 2 acres), and many homes are in excess of 100 feet from the street.

The town was also able to pave the entire length of Morgan Drive which was about a mile in length. I don't believe that Morgan Drive had been paved for at least 20 years. Those residents did express sincere appreciation with having a new road surface in front of their homes.

Rehabilitation of Utica Street

In late 2013, I was approached by an engineering consultant who was also a member of the Metropolitan Planning Organization (MPO) about the possibility of allowing them to assist the town in getting funding for Utica Street. Initially, I wasn't too eager because the Town of Terry had received funding for Utica Street several years prior. However, because of all the design deficiencies that needed to be addressed on Utica Street, the town ended up diverting the funds to Cunningham Avenue in lieu of losing these road funds after contemplating a strategy for more than two years for the completion of the rehabilitation of Utica Street. However, this consultant was confident that his firm could properly address all design deficiencies and secure funding to rehabilitate Utica Street. I told him that if he was successful in getting this done that I would bring the matter to the Board of Aldermen for their consideration and approval.

Well, this consultant made good on his word. The town tentatively received grant funding of more than $400K to complete Utica Street. During this particular MPO funding cycle, the Town of Terry was the only small town that received funding. However, this optimism of having received funding for Utica Street was indeed short lived. When the board realized that this was a 75/25 grant (the grant paying seventy-five percent of the construction costs and the town paying the remaining twenty-five percent) and that the town would be expected to pay the project design costs, the board of aldermen initially hesitated. I explained that design costs are generally not eligible for funding in most infrastructure projects. In previous similar rehabilitation projects, the town had paid design costs for the small town Hinds County grant completed in late 2010. In addition, because the north part of Utica Street also had some flooding issues, I suggested that it would be a better long term value added to our MPO grant funds investment that we have the engineering consultant include in his design measures to mitigate flooding issues along Utica Street as well. A couple of the board members also lived along Utica Street and had publicly and personally complained to me about flooding issues on their respective properties previously.

I honestly think that the root of the problem with this board's extreme antagonism regarding Utica Street was not money but that my political adversaries were determined not to see another infrastructure or other project be completed under my administration. I felt that the political establishment and other of my political adversaries were working through various of the board members to accomplish this. By this time, as hard as I had lobbied the MPO to receive the funds, I was mentally prepared to return the funds should this board decide that they did not want to approve paying the town's share of the construction costs or the design costs. I just wanted the board to publicly vote against this project and then deal with the political heat from the residents of Utica Street. As much as these behind-the-scenes political operatives wanted the board to do their bidding, these same operatives were usually nowhere to be found should the board members be in the unenviable position of having to deal with political backlash from the town constituency for not funding a project where the majority of the funds were essentially given. However, the Utica Street project just barely got approved.

As Mayor, I tried to learn something from every infrastructure project that we completed. And I had finally figured out how we could actually work within our general budget and get more of the streets paved on our own. I hunted down a number of grant dollars that were used to fund a number of infrastructure projects. However, I told this board on a number of occasions that a municipality cannot operate on grant funding alone. And as a board, we cannot continue to tell people we cannot accomplish the things that we were elected to do because we don't have the money.

But this board was going to hear nothing of the sort. I even had one of the board members personally tell me that in the future, if we couldn't get a one hundred percent grant that they would not vote for its approval. Talk about a welfare mentality.

I always said that I never wanted to be a Mayor and get nothing accomplished or be among any group of persons where I know I wasn't wanted. Sadly, Utica Street was my last infrastructure project as Mayor of the Town of Terry. It was officially completed in late September 2015.

The Terry Political Establishment

During the Republican Presidential Primaries of 2016, it was largely reported in the national media about the chasm within the Republican party between the establishment and its base. I think that a similar situation exists between the Town of Terry establishment and its base as well.

- **The African American Establishment**

There are a few long established African American families in Terry that I would say represent the political establishment. And I think that certain of the African American establishment wanted me out. Period. I was never their guy, and perhaps they felt that they couldn't depend on me to operate the way that they wanted. I never intentionally went against anyone. The nearest that I could ever figure out was that the African American establishment did not seem to want real, substantive progress for the Town. And I did. And therein was the root of the problem.

In my opinion, the black establishment made no effort to support any substantial infrastructure development in town. In some cases as I have previously described, the black establishment worked through some of the Board to stymie a number of much needed municipal infrastructure projects that would have been beneficial for all townsfolk.

- **The White Establishment Community**

There is a white establishment in Terry as well. In my opinion, the white establishment is largely represented by the First Baptist Church of Terry. However, the white establishment seems to be dying out. Their children either have moved away never to return and/or have no interest in maintaining the control that their white parents did in the previous generations. And I'm sure that the black establishment sees this, and their intention is to seize control of this community. And like some of the racist whites from times past, the intention of the black establishment seems to be to control and exploit this community to benefit them and their friends and exclude the rest, especially the white establishment.

I never took time to learn exactly who these people were and exactly what they wanted. In the end, that was to my peril.

• My General Thoughts on the Terry Political Establishment

As Mayor, an issue that I did have with both the black and white establishments is that a number of them actually lived outside of the town's political jurisdiction yet were very insistent on influencing and directing what went on within the town limits. In a lot of ways, they treated the town as its figurative mistress. They wanted the privilege of directing the town's agenda but were not interested in sharing in the financial responsibility as a legitimate resident. Things such as shouldering a fair share of the costs related to the town's maintenance and upkeep. They were most often interested in taking but reticent to give back. Both black and white establishment were all for the town extending its services to them outside of its corporate limits with no regard to costs of these services. And yet time and again, they were adamantly opposed to annexation which would have given legitimacy to this figurative common-law relationship. In my opinion, the invisible political establishment could not and should not have it both ways.

When I first became Mayor, I had no idea of the unwritten rules of Southern culture much less of this town. I had to learn that nothing happens in the most communities without the implicit or explicit blessing of the often invisible political establishment.

Now, I was not under the impression that I really had complete support of either black or white political establishment as Mayor. However, I would have to say that the African American establishment and the Hinds County Democratic Party have been more open with their disdain of me and their desire to replace me almost from day one. It could be that these groups just wanted to expand the Mississippi Democrat brand. Perhaps I wasn't of any use to either because I really didn't explicitly subscribe to either the Democrat or Republican brand. I was just the people's Mayor.

Folks, it's evident to me that this exclusionary, racist agenda didn't work for the white people when they were in control as evidenced by the absolute mess that I inherited when I became Mayor. And it's my belief that there is no reasonable expectation that these essentially racist, exclusionary tactics are expected to work for the African American leader, either. You cannot move any system forward when entire demographics in the community have been intentionally disenfranchised.

- **Grass Roots Movement for Mayor**

When I first ran for Mayor, it was a grass-roots kind of thing. I didn't consult the black or white establishment prior to my accepting the challenge to run. There was no intended disrespect or slight on my part. As a transplant from the Midwest and a political novice, I was just too ignorant of the unwritten rules and of politics to even know that's what I was supposed to do. My guess is that that many of the white establishment had grown weary of then Mayor William Pechloff and were looking for a change. As I had indicated, I had been asked to run for mayor three times before I finally agreed to run.

The African American community was tired of Mayor Billy Pechloff as well. And I think that the black establishment's candidate of choice was one of the other African Americans on the board other than me. My opinion is that the black establishment's choice of Mayor Pechloff's successor decided that he didn't have the backbone to stand up and run for mayor against a white man. Instead, both the other African Americans on the board made the safer choice to run again for alderman and thus have a better chance of remaining on the board.

When I ran for re-election as Mayor in 2009, the Hinds County Democratic Party put some guy up against me for election to be a spoiler. On this guy's qualifying papers, his listed a Jackson, MS address as his place of residence to run in a Terry, MS election. When his application was denied, the Hinds County Democrats took the matter to Court but in the end, they did not prevail. Please note that up until this time, none of the town's elections had had any kind of partisan participation or interest.

I sincerely believe that many persons within the State of Mississippi Democratic Party think that African American voters (who in Mississippi are overwhelmingly Democratic) are so naive that they will blindly elect anybody who has a "D" by their name. As insulting as this thinking may be, they may have a point when you look at how what happened in the 2015 Mississippi gubernatorial primary. A totally unknown guy received more votes and beat a candidate that the state Democrats thought was a shoe-in for the Democratic gubernatorial nomination. Incidentally, this gubernatorial spoiler guy was from Terry, MS. I believe that he said that he was so busy with his full-time job that even he didn't vote in the gubernatorial primary.

When I made my third run for mayor in 2013, the Hinds County Democratic Party put up another candidate to run against me. The guy that they ran against me had been on the town board and had previously run as an Independent. It was a fairly nasty, close election, but in the end, I was determined by the town municipal election board to be the winner.

The election was close, but it wasn't as close as it has been reported. In the 2013 election, the election board tallied all the machine votes which indicated that I was ahead. Then the absentee votes were hand tallied and added to the machine total which showed I was still ahead. Of the absentee ballots received, there were a number that had a technicality where the town clerk didn't do everything that she was supposed to do. In an effort to avoid a big, ugly court mess, I encouraged them to throw out the ones with a technical irregularity. A number of these were from people that I feel supported me. Had they been counted (I don't think they were ever even opened), I think this would have made my re-election in 2013 even more decisive.

My challenger and the Hinds County Democratic Party contested the election in Court. However, the Courts again ruled in my favor. The Board of Aldermen (a number of them related to both each other as well as my mayoral election challenger) were apparently were so angry over the election that they dismissed the entire municipal election board and for several months refused to approve payment for the attorney who defended the town in the election contest. (Because our municipal attorney at the time of the election contest was a blood relative of my opponent, I sought outside counsel for the election contest.)

Looking back on things, I think that I just didn't realize that politics is politics and often it is dirty regardless of the place. I think that I stayed in politics too long and was totally unaware and unprepared for what is typically the natural progression of politicians in politics. And being in politics as long as I was you acquire political enemies.

As I write these memoirs, the nation is in the midst of the presidential election of 2016. There were two significant issues that have rankled persons of both major political parties. During one of the presidential debates, one candidate indicated that he may not accept the outcome of the election. The second issue of concern is that this same candidate indicated that he would make every effort to put the other presidential candidate in jail should he win the election.

There was a big public outcry that questioning the integrity of elections and making threats to jail an opponent was considered by national pundits of both major political parties as essentially crossing the line of fairness and decency. Well, I'm here to say that both these things happened to me as a result of the 2013 Mayoral race in Terry, MS. As disappointed as I may have been about the election, if I had lost, I would have accepted it. And I have never had such animosity toward any human being that I would have used every bit of political clout in an effort to destroy another human being. So, what does this say about Mississippi?

I was very proud of the accomplishments that occurred under my administration. Most people approved of them as well. Although some did not. I felt that these naysayers would eventually get over it and get on board. I failed to realize that no matter what good that you may feel that you accomplish that there is always somebody out there who may have an agenda different than mine. And sometimes, these haters will do anything including mow you down if they feel that you stand between them and what they want.

• Robert Shuler Smith, Hinds County District Attorney

As I indicated earlier, these charges of embezzlement of $2,748.08 on the Town of Terry's credit card were originally presented to the office of Hinds County District Attorney. The Hinds County DA declined to pursue the case because the funds were re-paid when the matter was brought to my attention shortly after the election contest in August 2013. For reasons that I am still unclear about, the Hinds County DA recused himself. Let me say that I do not have a personal or close relationship with Mr. Robert Shuler Smith. However, his reputation long before he entered politics was that of a capable African American attorney.

However, in the process of putting the final touches on this memoir, it was reported in the *Clarion-Ledger* newspaper that the Hinds County District Attorney himself was indicted on misdemeanor and felony charges of aiding defendants in some type of criminal proceedings. The significance of this is that these charges potentially could result in the Hinds County DA himself be removed from his office.

First of all, let me say that I have no firsthand knowledge about the Hinds County DA's case or that I am that knowledgeable about the law in general. However, one thing that seems glaringly clear to me is how the same cast of characters that were involved in my case are now involved in this matter with charges against the Hinds County District Attorney. In my opinion, this is too much of a coincidence involving another smart, educated, capable and ambitious African American male and public official to ignore. I find it absolutely amazing that these organizations instead of being in support of one another are instead tying up valuable resources in an effort to take this well respected and duly elected African American official down.

I would like to say that I do feel that what this establishment culture of the State of Mississippi is trying to do to the Hinds County District Attorney is wrong. I also feel that what these same bad actors did to me as Mayor of the Town of Terry, MS was VERY wrong as well. Is this an effort to overturn a sovereign election? Again, what does this say about Mississippi that we sit back and let this happen to our African American public servants?

Are African Americans Unfairly Targeted by the State of Mississippi?

The Jackson International – Medgar Wiley Evers Airport is a public use airport operated under the auspices of a Board of Directors appointed by the City of Jackson, Mississippi. The Board is majority African American and reflective of the City of Jackson, MS. Apparently, the state legislature recently passed a law to alter the composition of the airport's Board of Directors. This matter has been hotly contested, with a majority of the African American state legislators as well as the City of Jackson in opposition to this move, and the white legislators in support of this legislation. Despite the controversy, Governor Phil Bryant recently signed this bill into legislation. This law will likely be appealed by those in opposition. In the meantime, this very public dispute will likely have negative economic consequences to our capitol City of Jackson, the airport, and to the state.

When you consider what is going on with African American men such as Hinds County DA Robert Shuler Smith, local OB/GYN Dr. Carl Reddix, myself (among others) and predominantly African American operated organizations such as the Jackson International – Medgar Wiley Evers Airport, it really makes me wonder. There does seem to be some kind of pattern here too obvious to ignore.

Some of the Challenges I Faced As Mayor

- ### The Agri-Bio Facility Proposal

Shortly after I took office in 2005, there was a Congressional proposal for an Agri-Bio Facility in the Sonny McDonald Industrial Park just north of Terry near the I-55 Wynndale exit. This was a large industrial park with almost no tenants. So, just to get occupants in the industrial park at the very least would be a step in the right direction and perhaps could positively influence the tax base of Hinds County.

The local effort for this proposal was led by the City of Jackson Chamber of Commerce, the Hinds County Economic Development District, Hinds County Board of Supervisors, and the University of Mississippi Medical Center among others. In layman terms, the Agri-Bio Facility proposal was a veterinary version of the Center for Disease Control (CDC) in Atlanta, GA. The other previously mentioned organizations of support had called and asked that as the Mayor of the Town of Terry that I write a letter of support. The lead proponents were in the process of scheduling a number of public meetings in Terry and other locations in Hinds County to inform and hopefully garner public support for this project. There were other metro-Jackson locations under consideration for the proposed agri-bio facility. However, the Sonny McDonald Industrial Park just north of Terry was definitely on their short list because they felt that this industrial park location could most easily satisfy the criteria that were required for such a facility.

Per the request of the Jackson Chamber of Commerce etc. al., I was more than delighted to write a letter of support as Mayor. The more that I thought about this proposal, the more that I thought that this could potentially be a game changer in the Town of Terry, in Hinds County, and even in the State of Mississippi. Perhaps, it could have an even greater impact upon the local and state economy as when Nissan North America was established in Madison County, MS.

Had this proposal materialized, it eventually would have included more than just the agri-bio facility itself. As a veterinarian research facility, it would likely have attracted pharmaceutical companies interested in working with this facility to develop drugs for treatment. These pharmaceutical companies in term would likely be interested in working with the local and state universities, etc. in various research efforts. Potentially, this facility would likely have attracted scientists, engineers, and other persons with technical backgrounds and expertise from all over the nation. I was truly excited about the possibilities of this proposal.

Shortly after the information meetings began in the Terry area, I was contacted by some of the local establishment essentially asking me to publicly rescind my previous letter of support of this proposal. The reasons that were given to me seemed to be based more on personal preference and less on substantive fact. My response was to remind them that I had only a few weeks ago had written a letter of support and that I was still very much in support of the proposal. Further, I felt that the other lead proponents would likely be willing to try to mitigate any concerns that they or anyone else might have regarding this proposal. Finally, I told them that I didn't really want to appear as indecisive as Mayor by publicly rescinding a position that only weeks earlier that I publicly wrote a letter of support for. But of course, this was my reputation, not theirs, to be concerned about.

I was by no means the lone hold-out in my support of this proposal. However, I was contacted several times by the establishment who were insistent that I rescind my letter of support. Finally, I told the establishment that while I could not write a rescinding letter, I would publicly stand mute on the issue and not issue any more statements positive or negative or contribute to the ongoing debate. Still, that did not satisfy the establishment in opposition to the agri-bio facility proposal.

I later on discovered that one of the board members wrote a letter in opposition to the project and apparently disseminated it. This board member had somehow gained access to my office without my knowledge and without my permission and obtained town stationery to pen this letter. It's my understanding that this board member did sign their own name. In addition to the manner in which it was done (somehow gaining access to my office without my permission and without my knowledge), it was not this board member's place to use town stationery for official matters. Period.

In the end, because the Town of Terry establishment was in opposition to this proposal and apparently had the ear of the Congressional delegation, it didn't happen. I believe that the facility was eventually located somewhere in the state of Kansas. Had the facility been established in or near Terry, I think it would have indeed been a game changer for the Town of Terry, Hinds County, and even to the State of Mississippi. I think that this action demonstrates that the collective establishment in Terry, MS was not seriously interested in significant change.

- **Northeast Terry Sewer Extension Project**

As if the election contest of 2013 wasn't enough political drama, some of the subsequent actions of some of the board members during the construction of the northeast municipal sewer extension project into northeast Terry were even worse.

During my second administration, I worked to get the $1.2 million ($600K grant, and $600 CDBG loan) to expand sewer service in this section of town. Initially, the entire board voted in favor of this sewer expansion project. However, once the grant was approved, a couple of the board members did everything that they could to sabotage this project. I had personally wanted to complete this project for years, and it was perhaps the most difficult grant to get approved that I had ever been involved with. And for certain of the board to work against this much needed effort was unconscionable in my opinion.

As with any type of government-sponsored infrastructure project, there is a lot of bureaucratic red tape and public meetings that are required prior to making application for funding or prior to receiving this funding. Essentially, the Capital Access Program (CAP) loan funding was to fund the sewer line for those residents whose income exceeded the income level that would have otherwise allowed them to qualify under the grant portion. And for the town to be able to receive these funds, a public meeting and a majority affirmative vote by the board was required.

One of the aldermen voted in opposition to proceeding with this sewer expansion project. I believe that the only reason that they decided to oppose the vote (after they initially voted to approve the Mayor to submit a grant application) was that this board member would have to cast their vote in a public meeting in front of white establishment. Some of these "establishment" white people would never support anything that didn't benefit them personally. The northeast Terry sewer project was essentially to bring service to a majority African American area of town. It's only common sense that at any given time, not all projects will benefit all communities because different areas have different needs. But hopefully, over time, some benefit will come to every community.

The other alderman in opposition was in my opinion just being led by those establishment persons who had instructed them to stymie any proposal at any cost because the establishment did not want another project completed under my administration.

Even more disappointing was that these aldermen encouraged as many of the other sewer project beneficiaries (who had previously submitted statements of support for this project) to refuse to grant the town an easement on their respective properties to permit placement of the mainline sewer. And this was all after the town had received approval for the $1.2 million in funding. This project came dangerously close to falling apart. I had to personally get with our public works people and perform some field re-engineering at certain critical points where pump stations were needed to ensure that this project could function as intended.

The municipal sewer extension project was like manna from heaven for the town because it included not just the construction of the sewer main line, but the service line up to each individual's home. This project was one hundred percent turn-key for the residents of northeast Terry. All installation costs associated with the sewer were included in the project. All the residents had to do was begin paying a sewer bill once installation was completed. For years, residents of northeast Terry had asked that municipal sewer services be extended to this area. However, the Board was hesitant to raise taxes sufficiently to cover the cost of this project.

Some of the reason that the level of services in much of Mississippi continues to be low is that leadership often fails to see the benefits of long-term vision, and in the short term, they just end up being penny wise and pound foolish. In the age of the West Nile, Ebola, and Zika viruses, who wouldn't jump at the opportunity of having an enclosed municipal sewer system in lieu of each resident doing their own thing with a septic tank or sewage treatment plant that in many cases had been improperly constructed and/or maintained which contributed to the likelihood of public health concerns?!

As part of this project, we had to get signed waivers/easements from each resident to permit the sewer project to proceed. However, at such time the town was to file these easements with the County Tax Assessor's Office, it was discovered that all of these documents had gone missing at City Hall. We looked high and low, but the signed easements were nowhere to be found.

Eventually, we re-issued duplicate forms and asked all the affected residents in the project area to complete, sign, and re-submit their copies. I personally delivered them to the Hinds County Tax Assessor's Office for filing. We never did find out exactly what happened. In addition to a handful of town staff, two of the five board members also had keys to the City Hall building were these documents were deposited. The time frame of this occurrence was shortly after the final decision of the election contest of August 2013 which confirmed me as Mayor. Let me say that I do not actually know how all these easements were lost. However, you can draw your own conclusions and speculation about what really may have happened to these original documents.

• Town of Terry Employees

While the vast majority of our employees with the Town of Terry were very hard working, loyal, and a real joy to work with, that was not the case with all of them. This is one area where I have to admit that I could have done a better job in formally documenting unprofessional behavior and job performance and perhaps been more proactive in getting rid of bad actors earlier.

However, I often found myself between a rock and a hard place because in the Code Charter form of municipal government in the State of Mississippi, the Mayor does not have unilateral ability to hire and fire. The Mayor can only make recommendation(s), but the ultimate action to hire or fire employees rests with the Board of Aldermen. Even though it is the Mayor that daily supervises and works directly with town staff. Also, in the Code Charter form of municipal government, the Board of Aldermen are not supposed to supervise or interfere with the Mayor in day-to-day operation of the town. That being said, I could certainly have done a better job at identifying bad actors among the staff as well as proactively handling volatile personnel situations before they got worse and became even more problematic. In retrospect, I allowed bad behavior to continue for way too long, and when I did try to put my foot down, some of the troublesome employees had learned how to effectively play me against the board. When an employee either can't or won't take constructive criticism to heart, in retrospect that should have told me that this person likely doesn't have the temperament or desire to perform the job that they have been assigned and/or hired to do.

Because we had no tax base, in many cases the town could not offer a more competitive salary to perhaps attract a higher caliber of employee. Oftentimes, the real problems did not arise out of a employee's inability to do the job. The most frustrating problems were employees who did not seem to make a sincere effort to perform a job to the best of his or her ability and/or constantly made excuses and refused to acknowledge when they fell short of fulfilling their basic job duties.

In this small town, many persons were related to one another and to various of the board members who themselves were related and/or had close personal relationships with each other and the staff. So the objectivity that you would expect of board members to make professional decisions wasn't there. In addition, the political nature of municipal government made it even more difficult to make unbiased, professional, fact based personnel decisions.

It's kind of difficult to employ a high caliber police officer and have him/her potentially put their life on the line for the town for slightly above minimum wage. As a result, most of our better police officers worked for the town part time and worked full-time for another employer where they received benefits such as health insurance and retirement. Essentially, what we had was a revolving door of good employees. They would be with the town for a few months and then move on when a better job opportunity presented itself. And I couldn't blame these officers for ultimately making decisions in the best interests of themselves and their families.

Several of the board members, the political establishment, and residents wanted top-notch service from the town but in most cases were resistant to implementing bold, progressive changes that might include long-term infrastructure investment for the town, increasing taxes to support these community services, encouraging business development to expand the town's tax base, and providing a more comprehensive benefits package including healthcare to prospective employees.

In those cases where town employees had been so derelict in job performance and sufficient documentation was provided to the board for them to take decisive action, there often wasn't enough support from board members to effect this change. As a part-time Mayor in a small town, there were just too many things simultaneously coming at me to just get bogged down and spend an inordinate amount of time on any single issue. On several occasions, I would bring a personnel matter with documentation to the board for their action. However, the board would harangue about making a decision for weeks, and then I'd find myself having to give time to some other emergency or matter with no real decision or resolution of the matter.

This board often publicly talked about their rights as a board and their desire for efficiency and reform, but their collective actions indicated otherwise. The board collectively was hesitant to tell their relative or friend that they had to go when the employee's job performance or professional behavior was clearly less than what it should have been. Even in those situations where the problem could not be ignored, this Board of Aldermen more often than not allow the politics to trump their jealously guarded right as a Board to act on my recommendation to terminate or take an adverse action regarding an employee. In several cases, they insisted that I alone (not with the Board) actually deliver bad news to an employee. They wanted it to be that it was the Mayor who delivered the blow. So the employee's subsequent anger and vitriol would be directed at me.

I found out the hard way that one person no matter how honorable their intentions cannot change culture of an entire community. In my more than ten years as Mayor, I cannot tell you how many knock down drag outs that I have had to referee between supervisors and employees, between board members and town staff, and even a few that wanted to attack me when I didn't give them the answer or support that they expected.

We had hourly employees who refused to come to work yet complained when their pay was docked. I had a very difficult time convincing some board members that hiring additional person(s) to assist an unproductive, incompetent employee in the end was both financially inefficient and counterproductive. In most cases, most bad actor employees eventually left of their own volition. There was a constant tug-of-war with this board philosophically of my not wanting to hire board members' friends and relatives and the board wanting to hire persons that I thought was clearly nepotism and in some cases an outright conflict of interest.

We had an hourly employee that became so fond of sleeping on the job that he had apparently brought a pillow from home presumably for comfort during his nap at work. This employee had simultaneously been running up the clock with a lot of overtime. I personally came upon this employee sleep in a closet at City Hall one weekend when I came up to catch up on some paperwork. I discovered this when I went into a closet to get something. This guy was so out of it that he never even woke up. I called his supervisor immediately, reported what had happened. After he was reprimanded, this employee began to harass a member of my family as retaliation.

A few weeks later, I personally witnessed this same employee during his duty time, out in his uniform in the town vehicle putting up campaign signs for my opponent in the upcoming election. Let me make it clear that no employee had ever been coerced into helping support my or anyone else's election. Secondly, all employees had been advised that canvassing during duty hours is strictly prohibited.

Through his supervisor, he was given the option of resigning or have the matter go before the full board with a recommendation of termination. This person resigned. However, this person continued his efforts to retaliate by reporting to the state wage and hour people that the town had paid him straight time in lieu of time and a half rate for any hours over 40 hours. This matter was actually from about two years prior. The Office of the Clerk had paid his overtime hours in straight time in lieu of time and a half hours. Because the town had committed a similar infraction in another matter previously, this time the town was issued a fine.

In another case, we had an employee who died unexpectedly. This person also had an insurance policy for which he had payments for his life insurance premium deducted by the town. In the process of this employee's family members making his funeral arrangements, his family was informed by the insurance company that his insurance policy had been canceled due to non-payment.

In another instance, the town had hired a contract firm to complete its annual audit. This practice of using a contract auditor had been in place long before I took office. As Mayor, I continued the use of a contract auditor because it did seem to work. It was the town's responsibility to provide all needed documents and copies to this contract auditing firm. One year, the original documents were mailed to the wrong address for the contract auditing firm. To compound this most unfortunate occurrence, the documents were mailed without the town's return address. Unfortunately, we never did locate the original documents despite repeated calls to the postal service requesting trackers for lost or misplaced mail. Because the documents that were lost were original documents, it took the Office of the Clerk months to rectify this mess.

I felt very bad about this entire matter. And unfortunately, when you deal with human beings, these kinds of things happen. And I do understand and had empathy for all involved.

In another instance, we hired an additional person in the Clerk's office to assist with certain bookkeeping duties. In addition, the town also hired a computer vendor/specialist person to organize and set up in the computer spread sheet things such as social security and other withholding, garnishments, etc. for each employee. Well, the contract auditor informs me that somehow these parameters had been manually changed for social security withholding after these parameters were set up by the software vendor. Apparently, there is some portion of social security deductions that are to be paid by the town and another part is to be paid from the employee's wages. According to the contract auditor, the withholding parameters had been clearly been changed to where the town paid both the town's portion and the employee's portion of social security withholding.

I did confer and ask both persons in the Clerk's office about how this could have happened. And neither one took responsibility. I couldn't prove or disprove anything or who did what.

However, I did relay the information given to me from the contract auditor to everyone in the Clerk's office that changing the percentage withholdings wasn't allowed, and that it wasn't to happen again once it has been set up.

I do feel that the State of Mississippi and the board of aldermen were unreasonably punitive toward me as Mayor in this matter. And although both the board of aldermen and the state became aware of were a number of instances where bookkeeping matters were not in compliance with state requirements, they ultimately pushed for criminal prosecution of the Mayor only.

I really cannot understand how the State of Mississippi came down on me so hard about $2,748.08 inadvertent misuse of a credit card. I never denied having used the credit card, and when brought to my attention, the town was promptly reimbursed.

However, no one can reasonably expect that as Mayor this was my specific job to accomplish these matters. I neither maintained nor mailed any of these documents. The Board was aware of this, yet there was no push by the Board or the state for prosecution in these matters.

In the end, I was the only one with the Town of Terry who was criminally prosecuted. These actions support my original premise that the local establishment, acting through certain of the Board of Aldermen, were looking for any way to ultimately overturn the 2013 Terry Mayoral election. Previous attempts to nullify the election had failed, and I think that this frustrated some persons.

TOWN OF TERRY

P. O. BOX 327
TERRY, MISSISSIPPI 39170-0327
TELEPHONE 601-878-5521
FAX 601-878-9501

OFFICERS

RODERICK T. NICHOLSON
MAYOR

MARY R. SMITH
CLERK & TAX COLLECTOR

ALDERMEN

VIRGINIA BAILEY
BONNIE HOLLY
APRIL MILEY
CONNIE TAYLOR
DORIS YOUNG

Date: September 23, 2014

To: Board Members

Re: Hiring Additional Person for Clerk's office

After some thought, it is my position that this board give consideration to not adding an additional part time person to the Town Clerk's office and water clerk assistant at this time. My rationale is as follows:

Consider financial obligations:
- Utica Street project
- Employee Health Insurance
- Additional person hired for the police department

I want to reiterate that I fully support all. However, they all have to be paid for. I think that the financial commitments that we've already made need to be given priority consideration to ensure that we are successful in meeting these obligations.

No Additional Administrative Personnel Are needed in the Water Department:
After speaking with the Deputy Clerk and Public Works Director, an additional person is not needed at this time. Although the Deputy Clerk works part-time, she is able to schedule her time off while simultaneously maintaining an acceptable level of service to the water and sewer customers. Why spend money on personnel that we really don't need?

The Clerk's Office Could Benefit More from Time Management Rather Than Additional Personnel:
Over this past year, the following actions have been taken to reduce the work load in the Clerk's Office:
- All water duties have been transferred to the Public Works Department.
- The Terry Police Department officers enter their own information in the LEAP program rather than have the Clerk enter this information. This has significantly reduced the Clerk's efforts in putting together the municipal Court docket.
- The Town uses a contractor that completes financial quarterly reports and other similar records. This has further reduced the duties required by the Clerk.
- In addition to her duties with the Public Works Department, the Deputy Clerk regularly substitutes for the Clerk at City Hall when the Clerk is not available. This averages 1-2 times per month.
- The Deputy Clerk continues to perform all the filing for City Hall.

Ideally, it would be preferable to have more personnel. However, additional personnel increases the Town's financial obligations. I recommend that we not add administrative staff at City Hall but instead focus on greater efficiency with the resources available. Thank you.

Rod

Roderick T. Nicholson
Mayor, Town of Terry

Description: Memo to the Board Advocating Training In Lieu of Hiring Additional Persons in the Office of the Clerk

Source: Memo Authored by Mayor Rod Nicholson

- ## The Terry News

When I first became Mayor in 2005, there was no local newspaper in operation in town. I met the publishers of what would eventually become The Terry News through the town's fledgling Terry Business Association. Their background was more in graphic arts than journalism. I suggested to them that they might consider publishing a local newsletter to help inform people about some of the more significant things happening in the Town of

Terry. I offered to write an article as a filler for this newsletter. Eventually, they agreed to publish the Terry Newsletter.

The relationship I thought went on in a fairly positive way for a while. The newsletter was distributed monthly via mail to everyone in town, and both the newsletter and my column seemed to have been well received by the community. Initially, I believe the cost of postage for mailing the newsletters was paid through the fees charged to various businesses and organizations that placed ads in the newsletter.

At some point, the publishers of this newsletter decided that in lieu of mailing their publication to individual residences and post office boxes, they would instead make their publication available at their various free newsstands throughout the community. This change may likely have been prompted by increasing costs to produce and mail the publication.

Shortly after their decision to cease mailing the newsletter, I received a number of calls from persons expressing disappointment about not being able to read my article each month. Many of those who did complain were elderly, and I presume they were less mobile to travel about town to find a newsstand that had the publication. About this same time, it was suggested that consider publishing my article in the *Byram Banner* which was also delivered by mail to each Terry resident. The *Byram Banner* is a similar publication that served Byram, a larger, recently re-incorporated community just north of Terry as well as the Town of Terry itself. When I contacted the publisher of the *Byram Banner* with this proposal, she was more than delighted to print my column. As a matter of fact, the *Byram Banner* had served the publishing needs for the Town of Terry prior to the existence of the *Terry News*.

After a couple of months, the *Terry News* publishers contacted me and gave me an ultimatum that either I cease concurrent publication of my article in the *Byram Banner* and the *Terry News* or they would not include my article in future issues of the *Terry News*. I explained to the *Terry News* publishers that since the *Terry News* was no longer mailed to homes in Terry that a number of elderly patrons, who comprise a significant portion of the town's population, expressed frustration of not being able to have access to read my monthly column. I also informed the *Terry News* publishers that other elected officials such as the state representatives regularly wrote articles and simultaneously placed them in both the *Byram*

Banner as well as the *Terry News* newspapers. So why my column should be handled any differently? I had been given no ultimatum or demand of publication exclusivity by the *Byram Banner* regarding placing my column in the *Terry News*. As a matter of fact, I placed my article periodically in other publications (with no adverse feedback) in the metropolitan Jackson, MS area to help promote what was going on in our town. I was told by the publisher of *Terry News* that I was solely being given an ultimatum because "I am the Mayor of Terry."

It was a difficult decision, but one of my goals as Mayor was to grow the Town of Terry. If we were going to in fact try to grow the town, we needed to let people outside of Terry know about some of the positive events and changes happening within our corporate limits.

I don't really know why the publishers of the *Terry News* were so adamant in their position. I don't know if their position was totally rooted in racism, but to some degree I do think that my race as an African American may have been a factor. Many people have a knee jerk reaction that African Americans, regardless of their position, education, or knowledge, are expected to respond in a subservient fashion to whites. I felt that as an African American, the *Terry News* publishers felt that it was not my place to ever take issue or question their position no matter how weak or flawed I may have felt their reasoning might be. Plain and simple.

At any rate, I really think that when I called the bluff of the *Terry News* and told them that if this was their ultimatum that I just wouldn't publish my article in the *Terry News*, they didn't know what to do. And I think that their pride would not allow them come to an African American and admit that they had handled this matter in such a wrong and disrespectful way. And although the publishers of the *Terry News* may have shored up support with some of the racists and some of my other political adversaries, I do know that their publication took some political heat as well because my article did add value to their publication and provided valuable information to those interested in the town. I heard from people all the time about how much they enjoyed reading my article each month. I suspect that there were other problems with the *Terry News*. Eventually, the *Terry News* ceased publication as such but was re-branded as the *Hinds County News*. The *Byram Banner* had a readership that was both larger than the *Terry News* and encompassed the Terry community.

I never published my article in the *Terry News* again. Essentially, I periodically free-lanced my monthly article about the Town of Terry to other local publications that included the *Byram Banner* and the *Jackson-Advocate*, another weekly publication that reports on news of interest to and affecting a largely African American population throughout the state.

Another Interesting Theory Regarding Black/White Relations in Mississippi

I have had several Mississippi native born whites tell me that many whites over a certain age in our state are almost certainly racist if they are from Mississippi. At first, I didn't believe it and asked why they would say such a thing. Their theory was that if they are a white Mississippi native and lived their formative years during the turbulent sixties, they would have to be racist.

As many of us are aware, many outspoken African Americans were literally run out of the state or worse just for speaking out against the racism of the state during this time. We all know about what happened with Emmett Till, the Freedom Riders Chaney, Schwerner, and Goodman, and Medgar Evers just to name a few. (According to their theory), what is less widely known is that there were also white Mississippians who stood up and spoke out against the racism and mistreatment of African Americans in Mississippi during this time. And these white persons were equally ostracized and run off and worse by the hard line racist whites as well.

According to this theory, those whites who remain in the State of Mississippi are essentially of two camps: 1) The unapologetic racist types, and 2) Those whites who are more docile, who know what goes on with the systemic treatment of the African American in Mississippi is wrong, but have been molded by their forefathers to either shut up or suffer the consequences of their white brothers who spoke out against the horrible treatment of African Americans during the Civil Rights movement. In my opinion, it's this former group that dominates the legislature today. And unfortunately, it's the former group that in many cases has formed a covert political alliance with many in the African American establishment in exchange for the token privileges or crumbs of influence that they have been given over the other African Americans in the state. With these alliances in place does indeed make affecting a change difficult in Mississippi.

Let me reiterate that this is a widely held sincere belief among far left whites, many native African Americans and conspiracy theorists in the State of Mississippi. As an outsider and someone who spent his formative years in the Midwest, I have to say that this is an interesting theory. What I do believe, though, is that the white people in Mississippi are not as monolithic in their thinking as many people nationally perceive them to be.

- **Tentative Bid to Run for Hinds County Board of Supervisors**

About a year after the hotly contested 2013 Terry Mayoral election, I was periodically asked by a number of professional and political associates in both Hinds County and state politics whether I would be interested in running for a seat on the Hinds County Board of Supervisors. I was flattered; however, I had just gone through a tough political battle in my re-election. There was also some speculation that the current supervisor in my district (Kenneth Stokes) had decided that he would like to return to his previous position as a Councilman with the City of Jackson, MS.

I was certainly flattered being asked by those persons that I had grown to have some respect and admiration for. However, having some sense of the negative side of politics, it was my realization of the distinct possibility that things could get ugly especially if there was some other person or constituency that had designs on occupying the position as well. Although I was flattered, I was adamant that under no circumstances would I run against Supervisor Stokes. However, I did indicate to those inquiring behind the scenes that if Supervisor Stokes were to voluntarily decide to leave the Board of Supervisors, that I would be open to consider a run for the Board of Supervisors. I had far too much respect for Supervisor Stokes and had such a disdain for muck racking politics to do otherwise.

Around late January/early February 2015, Supervisor Stokes did inform me that he was planning to return to the Jackson City Council and encouraged me to consider running for his old position. I expressed to Mr. Stokes my ambivalence for the reasons that I previously indicated. Mr. Stokes encouraged me to consider running for the BOS because his knowledge was that certain of the Terry establishment definitely wanted me out as Mayor of Terry and were willing to do anything that they could to ensure that I would not be re-elected as Mayor.

Supervisor Stokes also indicated that the Hinds County Board of Supervisors could greatly benefit from having a person of my talents, abilities, and temperament. He also indicated that as Supervisor, I would be in a better position to help the Town of Terry. Supervisor Stokes and others were very supportive and encouraging of me running. Supervisor Stokes stated to me personally that he would personally do all that he could to ensure that I carried that part of the City of Jackson within District 5. There were others supportive who indicated that they would support my candidacy should I decide to run. I told Supervisor Stokes and the others that I would seriously consider it.

At this point, I don't know who told who what, but it did get out that I was seriously considering a run for the Board of Supervisor position although I never formally or publicly announced my intentions. And then the strangest thing happened. I don't like to ever put much credence in any kind of gossip because that's just what it is. That being said, you certainly can't unhear something that you do hear. Around this time, it came back to me that certain of the Terry establishment were absolutely livid that I would even consider a run for the Board of Supervisors.

My instincts must be strange or off or something because for the life of me I was taken aback that anyone would react that way. There were some of my close constituents who did not want me to run but remain Mayor of Terry because they wanted me to continue the work that had begun under my administration, which I could understand. However, most of the feedback that I got was overwhelmingly positive. However, this good feeling was short lived because there was a strange, unexpected turn of events that in the end dictated that running for Board of Supervisors was not going to happen for me.

The Beginning of the End

Shortly after opponent's failed election contest in August 2013, I was contacted by the MS Office of the State Auditor regarding my use of the town credit card. Essentially, the State Auditor's Office's concerns were regarding charges from a couple of years earlier. I looked through the statements, and I did see five (5) charges for repairs to my personal vehicle. Originally, I agreed that they appeared improper and took full ownership of these credit card charges. I believe that they totaled around $2,748.08 (Two Thousand Seven Hundred Forty-Eight and 08/100 dollars) in total. Within 30 days, I had paid the amount that the Town Clerk and the State Auditor's Office indicated was owed. I paid the amount in question within thirty days of the State Auditor's initial inquiry. I didn't even question their figures; I just paid whatever they said that I owed. It was only after this became such a political issue that I would ultimately sit down and satisfy my own mind and conscience exactly what the circumstances were in this matter. After I provided the information to the State Auditor's Office, I didn't hear anything from anyone and just assumed that it had been handled to their satisfaction.

I later found out that in late 2014 that this matter was originally brought to the District Attorney for Hinds County where I reside. Because the money had been repaid and the town had been made whole, the Hinds County DA declined to prosecute the case and encouraged a civil resolution to this matter. Apparently, the Office of the Attorney General was not satisfied with the Hinds County DA's response and so pursued charges through the Rankin County Office of the District Attorney who issued the indictment against me. Because of all the things that had happened since 2013, I decided to seek my own legal counsel for this and any other matter should the need arise.

• **My Arrest**

As I indicated, I served as Mayor of the Town of Terry, MS. Like most small town mayors, on paper I was a part-time Mayor. I had full-time employment as a Civil Engineer with the USDOT-FAA at the Jackson International Airport. As Mayor of Terry, I worked a minimum of 30 hours weekly after work and on the weekends to ensure that the work of the town was properly executed.

Shortly after 8:30 am on Monday, March 30, 2015 I arrived at my place of full-time employment. As I exited my vehicle to begin my work day, I was approached by a number of law enforcement officers from the Rankin County Sheriff's Office who advised me that I was under arrest. I was surprised but did not resist. One of the guys from the Office of the State Auditor was there video recording the entire event.

The law enforcement guys handcuffed me, put me in the back of a Rankin County Patrol car and took me to the Rankin County jail. Unbeknownst to me at the time, this video guy from the State Auditor's Office immediately sent his recording to all the local news media and apparently it was shown during the mid-day news report.

Until I was formally arrested, neither my attorney nor I was aware that criminal charges were being pursued against me. Several months earlier, I had been issued a demand letter from the Office of State Auditor for $56K. At that point, and at my own expense, I retained an attorney for legal representation in this matter. Apparently, when they go back and conduct audits of this nature, they go back for 3 years.

Even if one were to consider every charge on the town credit card during this 3-year period, it would have been about $32K. And I certainly disputed the State Auditor's assumption that every charge on the credit card was improper. The difference between the Auditor's demand amount ($56K) and the total charges ($32K) were investigative fees, interest, and penalties. Eventually, I was charged with 5 counts of embezzlement in the amount of $2,748.08 all of which I had been completely reimbursed the town within 60 days after this matter was brought to my attention in August 2013 shortly after the trial for the election contest. I provided certification prior to my indictment.[2] These embezzlement charges essentially stem from my use of the town's credit card for repair expenses to vehicles that I used in conducting the business of the town.

Upon reflection on this matter, this is why I feel that the State Auditor and Rankin County's law enforcement handling of this matter was so wrong. If the Office of the State Auditor by statute has no arrest power, then why were they present on the parking lot to film my arrest? I had no knowledge that any kind of criminal proceeding was being conducted against me. My then-attorney had previously met with representatives from both the State Auditor and Attorney General's offices prior to my arrest. It was my belief that the entire matter was politically motivated in an election year where the politicians from these state offices were in tight political races where they perhaps felt themselves to be vulnerable. For whatever reasons and at the request of my initial attorney, I never attended any of these negotiation meetings.

It has NEVER been adequately explained to me why the Rankin County Sheriff's Department had to arrest me at my place of full-time employment. I wasn't avoiding or hiding from anyone. Both the State Auditor and the Attorney General offices were aware of and had prior communications with my legal counsel. According to my attorney, he was just as unaware as I was that criminal charges were being considered.

And even if charges were being considered, they could have come to the Terry City Hall, they could have come to my home, or they could have contacted my attorney. Rankin County Sheriff's Office could have contacted Hinds County Sheriff's office (where I reside) for them to serve the warrant. However, none of these options were apparently considered. Does anyone honestly believe had I been white that this matter over $2,748.08 that had already been paid would have been handled this way? I truly felt that this was done to embarrass, malign, and humiliate me solely for the political benefit of those persons up for re-election in statewide office.

---

[2]   *In December 2014, I ended up paying an additional $283 because apparently there was some discrepancy/communication issue between the Auditor's Office and our Town Clerk. I was indicted by the Rankin County DA's Office in March 2015.*

• **Indefinite Suspension from Full Time Government Job**

Shortly after this arrest and the subsequent public attention that ensued, I was suspended from my full-time job for several months without pay. Up to this point, I had been employed with the federal government for more than 29 years, including 25 years with the Federal Aviation Administration (FAA) with an exemplary work record of distinction. What made this matter even worse was that at that time, I was the sole financial provider for my family. Having a mortgage, trying to financially assist children in college, and just otherwise running a home with no income created a significant financial hardship for my entire family.

From April 2015 until July, 2015, I continually pressed my attorney to meet with the State Auditor and State Attorney General offices to try to resolve this matter. I was insistent that I felt that the majority of these credit card charges were indeed legitimate. I wanted to have a face-to-face meeting to discuss this matter and hopefully come to some kind of resolution. My attorney told me that both offices were unwilling due to the fact that both the leaders of the these offices were in the throes of respective hotly contested re-election campaigns. And apparently politicking on the campaign trail had priority consideration for them rather than resolution of these charges against me. My attorney had suggested that these guys might be more agreeable to negotiations after their respective primaries were concluded in August 2015.

I have to say that I've never been good at picking up on certain clues or the subtlety of what the hidden agendas of others might be. Although I was technically a Mayor, I focused my efforts more on the technical aspects of infrastructure and improvements in services to the town and less on the politics. And this was much to my peril in the long run.

But still, around July, 2015 I knew something was very wrong. But I just couldn't put my finger on it. There was just something all around about how this case had been handled. Having never personally dealt with the Courts (much less Rankin County Court), I had nothing to really compare it to. I want the reader to know that while I admit that I can be a bit ignorant about some things, I am not a stupid person. And historically when I sense something is amiss, more than likely the true reason(s) will eventually be revealed to me.

Around this time, the original judge assigned in this case, Rankin County Circuit Court Judge John Emfenger, recused himself from the case. I believe that Judge Emfenger's reasoning offered was that his daughter was an employee of the State Attorney General's office who was prosecuting this case. However, prior to Judge Emfenger's recusal, because I technically did not enter a plea by the prescribed date according to the schedule, my only options going forward with a new judge were either to enter an Open Plea or take the case directly to trial.

Also around this same time, I decided to change legal counsel. The actual day that Judge Emfenger recused himself my new counsel was supposed to be present and formally advise the court of the change in counsel. However, my new attorney was delayed in traffic. A representative from the attorney general's office was present as well. Rather than call the case later, Judge Emfenger proceeded and advised me that I should so inform my attorney about options moving forward on a case that he (Emfenger) advised from which he would be recusing himself. Not being an attorney and totally being unfamiliar with Court proceedings, it was all a blur at the time. All I wanted to do is get some remedy from this situation and get back to the natural order of my life.

Although I am not an attorney, I do, however, understand the concept of recusal. Recusal is essentially when someone does not participate because of some perceived prejudice that their participation might present. And if Judge Emfenger's daughter worked in the AG's Office, I think that his recusal was likely warranted. However, I don't think that Emfenger had any right to dictate what option(s) should be available to any future proceedings. But that is exactly what I feel Judge Emfenger did. And I also feel that the new Judge (William Chapman) willingly participated in this. In my opinion, on paper Emfenger did recuse himself. But in practice, I have doubts whether Judge Emfenger may have channeled his opinions through Judge William Chapman. It may or may not have been inadvertent. But this is Rankin County, Mississippi.

• Rankin County, Mississippi

I had heard stories about Rankin County for years. For those persons who may read this book who live outside of Mississippi or are unfamiliar with Rankin County, I would suggest that you Google the name Deryl

Dedmon. In 2011, Mr. Dedmon, a young white man, and some of his friends, apparently on a number of occasions would come over to Hinds County, a predominantly African American community, and harass African American persons. On the night of June 26, 2011, Dedmon and a group of his friends came over to Hinds County robbed and brutally murdered a Mr. James Craig Anderson by repeatedly beating Anderson and running over him with his vehicle. The entire event was recorded by the hotel camera in the parking event where this situation unfolded. Mr. Dedmon eventually pled guilty to this heinous hate crime.

I have talked to African American co-workers who indicated that they were harassed at traffic stops while driving to and from work through Rankin County. Other African American acquaintances who worked in Rankin County indicated to me instances of blatant discrimination that they endured in their respective workplaces. After what I experienced on March 30, 2015, I can certainly believe that this is entirely possible and even likely eventually for an African American in Rankin County, MS.

I sincerely believe that a LOT of things happen here, a LOT of people get railroaded by the system far more often than a lot of people might believe here in Mississippi. And even today, it's often done so openly, and the persons who perpetrate these injustices are more aware than ignorant of the consequences on others of what they are doing. I don't think it would be difficult for a trained legal organization with resources and an absence of bias (such as the USDOJ) to clearly spot deliberate patterns of discrimination and harassment. Because of its nationwide reputation, many people feel that it's hopeless and choose not to get involved. And this works to the perpetrators' advantage. This effectively keeps things closed. And if the outside people don't come in and press these issues, things may never change. People need to remember that an end to blatant racial discrimination did not happen here in Mississippi until the Federal government came in and forced a change despite changes in the law. And that was only 50 years ago. These views take a long time to die in a closed society. We need help!

I do not know the ins and out of the law or the legal system. However, I felt very deeply about how wrong this matter was handled. Several weeks before I was sentenced, I wrote a letter to the US Department of Justice office and suggested that they need to come in and look for patterns of racial abuse and discrimination by certain agencies in the State of Mississippi.

As Mayor, I had heard of a number of cases similar to mine where people were just railroaded. I didn't know the particulars of these cases, but I did feel that the persons sharing their stories with me were sincere. Having lived in Mississippi for a number of years, I have seen how people on the highest level in the legislature do and allow things that seem so blatantly unfair, that they make no common sense whatsoever, but the rank-and-file either can't or doesn't do anything about it. And as always, African Americans seem to be disproportionately represented as a group on the receiving end of these discriminatory practices. I sent my request to the USDOJ via certified mail. However, I received a response from the USDOJ via letter dated April 23, 2016, several months after my December 7, 2015 sentencing date. Essentially, the response from the USDOJ was a form letter of acknowledgement and offered no real remedy to my predicament.

However, when my new attorney received his paper work through Rankin County Circuit Court, there was no specific mention of an open plea or trial being the only avenues by which to proceed forward. At that time, both my attorney and the attorney from the Attorney General's offices even began to negotiate a plea agreement.

In early November 2015 I cannot tell you how emotionally tired and drained I was in dealing with this matter. I was just ready for this matter to be resolved. Reluctantly, I agreed to the plea agreement negotiated between my attorney and the AG's office. As we were going through the proceedings in Court, the court reporter whispered something to Judge William Chapman. This woman used a book or paper of some sort to shield her conversation with Judge Chapman. Judge Chapman then decided that he was not going to accept the plea agreement and cited what the previous judge (John Emfenger) had said regarding the options of open plea or trial. Judge Chapman then publicly suggested that I had personally attempted to manipulate my attorney by not advising him of this matter.

It wasn't until after I had been sentenced that clarity had come to me exactly why I didn't agree with Judge Chapman's accusations. How am I supposed to know all the subtleties of the law enough to manipulate anyone? The paperwork sent from the Rankin County Court to my new attorney did not mention it. A representative from the AG's office, Stanley Alexander,

(who is also an attorney) was present at the time when this conversation occurred. And yet HE (Alexander) entered into negotiations with my attorney working toward a plea agreement. Essentially what was said in Court was not in agreement with the subsequent paperwork that followed. And that in my opinion was the root cause of any misunderstanding of what the proceedings were to be. My new attorney indicated to me that he agreed that the paperwork nor any conversation between himself and the AG's office never specifically mentioned the only options to remedy this case were an open plea or taking the case to trial. I don't know why my attorney did not expound this point on my behalf to the court.

Why I Used the Town Credit Card for Personal Expenses

First of all, I would like to say to everyone that I am deeply sorry for the confusion and the fallout that this entire matter has created for the Town, my family, and for me. The reader or casual observer may not understand what it is like to be a Mayor in a small town with often limited resources. I was elected Mayor and presided over the time under three separate administrations. During the first administration, I used my personal vehicle for countless things for the town and neither asked for nor received any compensation in the form of mileage, fuel, or insurance for my vehicle. As a matter of fact, I served as the Resident Engineer in the construction of the new City Hall building. The Town didn't have the money to pay our engineer-of-record (Southern Consultants, Inc.) As a Civil Engineer, I had the skill set to accomplish the task, and I was more than happy to help the town out. I could have charged mileage because I did use my personal vehicle for all kinds of things during the city hall construction project. But, I never did. It's rather ironic that there were no board members fired up demanding that I be reimbursed during the City Hall construction project accomplished during my first administration.

In my second term, I told the board that while I didn't mind helping the town out that I wasn't going to continue to give all my services away for free. After all, I made less than $500/month after taxes for the job of Mayor. So it wasn't that I was receiving a great compensation, anyway.

During my second term as Mayor, I personally wrote up a grant and secured funding to construct a new library building to replace the single-wide dilapidated trailer that served as the town's original library. Because the proposed building was on 16th Section land, I negotiated the lease with both the school board and the Secretary of State's offices. I personally negotiated an agreement favorable to the town with the architect to produce a set of plans suitable for bidding and construction. Again, in

order to put more of the money into the construction of the project and because of my success in serving in this capacity in the previous town construction project (City Hall), I served as Resident Engineer on the library construction project as well.

However, I did decide that I would at least charge mileage for using my personal truck during the library construction project. This was in 2011. The project took about 6 months to complete. I used a base figure of $0.50/mile[3]; my total mileage reimbursement should have been $3,600.00. Toward the end of the construction project, I had some repairs on my vehicle (the tires and another mechanical repair) that were about $1,500.00. I felt that these repairs were justified because 90% of the miles on this vehicle during this time was for the library construction project. In my mind (at the time), I thought it was fair to both me and the town to charge the town $1,500 in lieu of $3,600 which I was entitled to for mileage reimbursement. So, that's why I did it. No other money between the town and me ever changed hands. I truly felt that I had been fair, and I didn't think anything more about this. I submitted the credit card payment to the Clerk's Office, it was paid, and I never even thought about this matter until it came up in late August 2013 shortly after the election contest.

What I just described to you I had totally forgotten about at the time this matter was brought to me in late August 2013. I now realize that should have kept better records. I was so busy and so stressed out from going through the election contest and keeping City Hall running properly. And not let us forget that I had a full-time job from which I derived most of my financial sustenance. So the details didn't come back into my mind until much later. The reader has to understand that I was in the throes of dealing with a hostile board that for almost six months refused to pay the attorney who successfully defended the town in the election contest. Call me naïve (which I was), but it wasn't until this matter that I realized that I had a majority of the board who was against me and had counted on my not receiving a third term as Mayor. The majority of the aldermen on the

---

[3]   The mileage rate calculation that I used ($0.50/mile) is actually less than the 2011 mileage rate from IRS Publication IR-2011-69 dated June 23, 2011 which was $0.555/mile).

board were related to each other as well as to my political opponent in the election. Please note that the town municipal attorney, was not the attorney who defended the town in the election contest. Our town attorney was related to my opponent in the election contest as well as at least two of the Aldermen on the board.

When this matter about the personal purchase on the credit card was brought to my attention back in August 2013, I was somewhat surprised myself. I have never denied having made the purchases. I took ownership, and I immediately made restitution to the town. And when you think about it, by my reimbursing the town (rather than explaining the circumstances of these purchases) I did myself a disservice. Rather than getting fairly reimbursed for the use of my vehicle in service to the town, I instead gave even more of services away to the town.

About the same time in August 2011, and in a similar way, there were purchases on the credit card for my other personal vehicle. I used this vehicle in picking up, transporting trees, hedges, and other plants either given to the town outright or at some reduced cost through my participation in the Mississippi Urban Forestry Council. I served as the State President of this organization during most of the ten years that I served as Mayor of the Town of Terry. As state president of this organization, I was able to get many trees, plants, crepe myrtles, and other plantings for the beautification of the town. These trees and plants were placed in the Village Square Park across from City Hall, in front of the new City Hall building, along Cunningham Avenue, and at various points at the Terry High School campus. I used my other vehicle because it had an enclosed hatch which better protected live plants from wind shear in transport. As president of the MS Urban Forestry Council, I also used my vehicle to go from Terry to the Reservoir, to Canton, to Pearl, to McComb, to Jackson, to a number of conferences and attend meetings all over the state. Again using the same mileage figure of $0.50/mile my total mileage using my personal vehicle for this organization over about 8 months was about $1,300.00. I had repairs to this vehicle that were less than that, so I just charged the cost of these repairs on the town credit card. And again, I was not reimbursed for mileage but instead charged an approximate equal amount on the town credit card.

If I had it to do over, I may have been better off just charging the higher mileage figure, and charged the repairs to my own credit card or through other personal means. In my mind from a paperwork standpoint, it was just simpler to do it this way. (In my mind at the time), I thought by doing it the way that I did could get the matter accomplished without all the paperwork. In this case, I was certainly penny-wise and pound foolish.

But do I understand how one just looking at a credit card bill might look at this suspiciously? Absolutely. And rather than just pay the bill, I should have taken the time to wrack my brain and my notes to formulate a reason to explain why I did what I did. In handling it the way that I did, I certainly contributed to the suspicion/confusion in this matter.

One time, I made an attempt to explain to this Board of Aldermen about the circumstances regarding the credit card purchases. However, I really don't think that they were open to hearing anything other than what they wanted to believe. By then, it was apparent to me that this board had an agenda to take absolute control of City Hall and that there were no plans for me to be a part of it.

I had discussed this matter with my original attorney. He indicated that the less said to the Board the better considering that they were hostile and their possible agenda(s). I took his advice.

But was what I done criminal? I really don't think so. In my heart, I know that wasn't the intention. Deep down, I don't think that even my political adversaries truly feel that way. But this was their opportunity to malign me and a convenient excuse that they had long been searching for to get me out of City Hall. They were so bitter about the outcome of the election and were apparently willing to do ANYTHING to overturn the 2013 Mayoral election and get their intended candidate in office. I'm almost ashamed to admit that it was right about this time when it dawned on me that being the Mayor is a political position with all the ramifications positive and negative that "political" implies. Prior to this, I just viewed myself as a person with a skill set in a small town just advocating for creative ways to move the town forward.

Actually, I'm not so sure that I didn't provide some documentation for the files. I know that I did the analysis, but other than my word and that it is generally accepted by everyone that I served as the town's pro bono resident engineer and spent a lot of time at the job sites during these construction sites and got a number of things for the town through the MS Urban Forestry Council. It's generally accepted that I affected these changes. The proof is that the buildings were constructed, I was there on the sites almost every day including weekends. And there is evidence throughout town (at the Village Square Park, at Terry High School and along the rights-of-way) of numerous trees, bushes, and flowers planted that the Board of Aldermen know that the town did not pay for.

I looked through the files for my personal notes, but I didn't see them. But then, there were MANY cases of papers and other information that somehow got lost. The Office of the Town Clerk was very disorganized. I can say how more than 50 signed easements simply came up missing prior to being filed with the Hinds County Tax Assessors office as part of our northeast Terry municipal sewer expansion project. I have previously described how a deceased employee's life insurance had somehow lapsed despite this employee having faithfully had the premiums deducted from his pay. I have described how an entire year of audit information was lost when the originals were mailed to the wrong address and this package didn't have the town's return address.

I can't emphatically say the same thing happened in this case with the documentation for these credit card purchases. But I can say that why is it that I am pursued criminally when other acts of gross negligence and incompetence with town personnel are simply ignored by the Board of Aldermen as well as the State of Mississippi?

I listened more to the people who were in support of me (which was the majority) and what I was trying to do and less to my detractors and haters. There had always been a few who were kind of your-friend-today-only types. I was somewhat aware of whom they were, but it never occurred to me that I had made anyone this angry or were capable of being so vindictive and hateful to resort to the tactics that they did. I had absolutely no idea.

Board's Assertion That They Had No Knowledge of Credit Card?

Baloney!

I do not agree with the Board's assessment that they apparently gave to the State Auditor that they had no knowledge of my use of a town credit card. I distinctly remember several of the board members instructing the Office of the Clerk to charge their hotel charges for the annual Mississippi Municipal League Conference on this exact credit card.

It was the Office of the Clerk who paid the bills, and it this office's responsibility to make sure that all bills were presented. As I have said, the Clerk's Office certainly wasn't the most organized. The Town of Terry was your typical a small town with limited and often poorly trained staff, I periodically helped when I could and where it seemed to be needed.

Actually, there were a number of instances where the credit card came in handy. For instance, I got a call one afternoon from the deputy clerk frantic that all of a sudden that the phones, faxes, and computers in the new public works building had suddenly stopped working. I then contacted the Office of the Clerk who insisted that these bills had been paid.

I then contacted the telephone company. They indicated that one of our accounts had a surplus (overpayment). But the other accounts were delinquent going on a couple of months. Essentially, how could this be?!

After going down to City Hall and pouring over this matter, and a few conversations with the woman who completed our annual audit, I finally realized what was going on. As I earlier indicated, the town had several telephone accounts through our telephone provider. And one of the things that the Clerk's Office did was that they would total up all the telephone accounts and mail one bill instead of making a check out for each separate account. Well, the problem was that each account has a different account number. I assumed that the Town Clerk would send only one invoice with the combined check. Although this combined check would be applied to only one of the accounts.

When we got to the root of the problem, I then asked the telephone company to apply the surplus to the delinquent accounts. Well, it just doesn't work that way with some businesses. I asked, "So what is the remedy to this dilemma? People are in the middle of work that I have mandated be completed in a prescribed period of time?"

Well, the Town Clerk could write out another check, but the mail won't go out until the following day, and would not likely work its way through the phone provider's system for about five business days not including the weekend. However, these employees needed to be productive now. I pulled out the credit card, and often paid the minimum to get everything back on. Within minutes after the credit card transaction had been completed, the phones, faxes, and computers were back on allowing the employees to resume their work.

All the details had been explained to the Board, so this again proves that they were either mistaken in their recollection or lying about not having any knowledge of a credit card. During our monthly board meetings, the Board was certainly aware of and observed how poorly put together the bills often were by the Office of the Clerk (and this same Board often complained to me about such). And although I was sympathetic to this situation and offered help where I could, this was merely using me as a political scapegoat as part of their larger agenda to undo the Terry mayoral election of 2013. Had this matter gone to trial, perhaps some of these facts would have been fleshed out. I indicated earlier ultimately why my attorney recommended that we not take the case to trial. At the time, it all made sense not to go to trial, and by this time, I was sick and tired of the harassment and constant conflict from this board.

Some of the Board members may have been so ignorant and uninformed and not even had taken the time to consider the facts or the context in which these matters occurred. Some didn't want to know but had merely aligned themselves with the forces of the political establishment for their own political benefit who simply wanted me gone from City Hall.

We certainly could have run a tighter ship at City Hall. However, under my administration, we actually did manage to get some things done.

In politics, there is an establishment of persons that operates invisibly. Essentially, many politicians take their direction and cues from this establishment. And the establishment in Terry simply did not want change and/or they didn't want the aggressive change that I advocated. As pitiful as the state of the town was, it was inconceivable to me that any group of persons could find the conditions that I saw when I first became mayor acceptable. It took me a long time to see this.

I think that this Board of Aldermen were either related to and/or understood the establishment politics and went along with it (presumably to secure their political support by the establishment) much better than I. I didn't realize this until I was being attacked full on. It took me a minute to even figure out where these "invisible" attacks were coming from. Had I realized this was the establishment's position and understood to what lengths the establishment was willing to go to maintain the status quo of the town, I may have decided not to run for a third time at all. However, I certainly don't apologize for the things that my administrations managed to accomplish. This could very well have explained why persons who initially feigned support but toward the end who seemed to almost daily manufacture reasons to paint me in such a negative light. If that's the instructions that the Board had been given by the town establishment and other political operatives, then that could explain the sudden shift in the political winds against me. Had this matter gone to trial, perhaps some of these facts would have been fleshed out.

Why I Plead Guilty

For more than a year and a half after this entire credit card matter was brought to my attention, I did everything that I humanly knew and was advised by my attorney's to do to resolve this matter. I literally spent more than $20K in attorney fees for a job that paid less than $500/month.

Please note that I did NOT want to plead guilty. I wanted to take the matter to trial. However, I plead guilty for the following reasons:

- <u>My attorney recommended pleading guilty</u>. My attorney indicated to me that he had tried cases through Rankin County, MS before, and in his estimation that this court was not likely to be fair to an African American, in particular one who is also an elected official. According to my attorney, my chances were greater than 95% that in a jury trial, I would get an all-white jury who would likely not be sympathetic or just.

- <u>My attorney indicated that he didn't have enough time to prepare for a trial.</u> When my attorney took the case, his estimation was that 5 charges in the amount of $2,748.08 wasn't really worth it from a time effort for either him or the State to pursue through a full blown trial. And considering that I had no prior criminal record, he felt fairly certain that he could reach some kind of plea agreement.

- <u>My attorney didn't think that the Judge would agree to continue the case in order to properly prepare for the trial.</u> My attorney indicated that his experience with the Judge presiding in my case was that this judge would not be flexible in granting extensions of any type. I found this point particularly troubling considering

THE FIRST BLACK MAYOR OF TERRY, MS

I thought the courts were set up to allow all persons every opportunity for a fair trial.

- <u>Money</u>. Because of my arrest in March 2015 at my place of full-time employment, I was suspended from my job for several months without pay, and so I hadn't paid my attorney in full when he agreed to take my case. Preparing for a trial would definitely involve additional resources. The reader has to understand that if the matter was taken to trial, it would have taken place in early December 2015.

Although I was eventually made whole financially and allowed to return to work in late September 2015 by my full-time employer after arbitration, it came too late to be of any benefit in these legal matters. I wasn't made whole until November 23, 2015. This is the day that I had to either enter an open plea or proceed to trial. And decision time for the logistics in preparing for a trial would have to come prior to this date.

My Reflections and Thoughts on Other Punitive Actions Taken By This Board of Aldermen

By the third time that I had been elected Mayor, I think that I had made decisions that although they did push forward my vision for the town and were well received by the vast majority of the community, I had also made a number of political enemies. And essentially, I had no plan in place to counter the political adversaries. I naively thought that the Board would appreciate the improvement in town services and infrastructure where just a few years prior there was none. I truly failed to look at the politics of it all. And my political enemies got the ear of the board members. I think that the board decided that it might be beneficial for them politically to throw me to the wolves. It may have not been that calculated, but I feel that's what happened.

• **Canceling the Mayor's Bond**
Shortly after my arrest in Rankin County, the board somehow decided that my bond wasn't necessary. Despite my having almost single-handedly written up grant justifications for funding the city hall, library, fire station/ public works building, paving of Cunningham Avenue, Utica Street, Morgan Drive, and Southfork Estates subdivisions; comprehensive water and sewer expansion projects. This board didn't do any of the leg work. And often rallied against the projects after funding had been obtained. I think that this board felt that that making a decision to cancel my bond would effectively end my term as Mayor. I often wondered how they would consider cancelling my bond when every mayor previously was bonded by the town. In the end, it was determined that while having a bond for the mayor was desirable, it wasn't an absolute requirement to occupy the office of the Mayor.

- **Hiring of Town Attorney**

Some of the problem that I had with former attorney was that I felt that he wasn't as impartial as I would have hoped that he could have been. I'm not necessarily saying that he was a bad person. However, he was related to at least two of our board members, and on a number of occasions, I really questioned his impartiality regarding a number of issues with this fractured, dysfunctional board of aldermen. And hiring another attorney in the same mold in my opinion would likely yield more of the same. Essentially, all I asked the Board of Aldermen to do was that we should select a municipal attorney that both the board as well as I could live with. As Mayor, I would have much more official day-to-day interaction with a town attorney than the Board of Aldermen would. So, I did feel that whoever this person would be should be someone that I felt comfortable working with.

I never had anything personal against this candidate's ability as an attorney. I was up front with the Board that I was absolutely against hiring this person for a number of reasons. I felt that their hiring would be nepotism.

As a matter of fact, I issued a veto action against hiring of this person for the reasons that I have stated above. And this entire Board of Aldermen voted unanimously to override my veto. This person was well aware that I didn't support their appointment as municipal attorney, and I do think that they understood how nepotism could be particularly problematic. I didn't necessarily insist that the Board rubber-stamp my personal choice but that we as a board choose someone that both the board and I could mutually support.

Cancelling of Health Insurance for Employees

I have gotten to know a number of our staff very well during the 10 years that I served as Mayor for the town. A number of them I would say were very dedicated, hard working, and gave 100 percent every day despite the low wages that they were paid. Most of them told me personally that they appreciated all that I tried to do for them. And over the years, it pained me terribly that the town did not offer its employees health insurance. When the financial condition of the town improved, I asked the board that in lieu of a cost of living increase provide health insurance for the employees. I had queried the staff about this proposal, and they were 100 percent in support of having paid healthcare in lieu of a paltry cost of living adjustment.

Anyone who is knowledgeable of health care knows that prevention is key to minimizing health care costs. Prevention includes such things as regular medical checkups, giving medicines to keep conditions such as hypertension, diabetes, and chronic illnesses in check from getting too far out of control.

It really bothered me to see dedicated employees develop serious medical issues that likely could have either been prevented or minimized with preventive health care monitoring. During my ten plus years as Mayor, I have personally witnessed employees have heart attacks, and have massive strokes that resulted in medical disability requiring long-term, extensive nursing home care, and even premature death from heart complications and cancer. All of these were men were less than 50 years of age. When these issues arose, the employees' only avenue of treatment was in the emergency room of the public hospital in Jackson.

However, for a brief period of time we did provide the town employees with health, dental, and vision insurance. Even for a small town it was expensive. However, there were problems. First of all, the payments were not delivered from the town to the healthcare service provider in a timely manner. Secondly, for whatever reason(s), the Office of the Clerk was not in support that the employees have insurance, and as such, the board members were often aggravated about the healthcare expenses.

The last that I checked, the Office of the Clerk is NOT a board member, and as such should have had no input into policy making decisions of the board. But among people in a small town, it's the unofficial (rather than the official) relationships that people consider. In my opinion, this illustrates that this Board of Aldermen were collectively far too flawed to effectively operate in a capacity of public service to a community. And because of this fundamental dysfunction, its' my opinion that many decisions made by this board were absolutely not in the town's or its employees' best interests.

And if you are wondering why didn't I do more assertion of my position as Mayor? In the Code Charter form of government here in MS, the Mayor cannot independently hire or fire. So there were MANY situations that I felt were truly wrong that I simply had to put up with.

As Mayor, I tried to show leadership by standing up for and by my convictions. And healthcare for the employees was one such issue. Of course, because I was an advocate of providing the employees health insurance and the relationships between the board were so antagonistic that this was just the excuse that they (Board members) needed to do everything that they could to vote to end health care insurance coverage instead of working together as a board to figure out a way to provide our employees who were so dedicated to and worked so hard to provide the best healthcare insurance that we could to them.

RODERICK T. NICHOLSON

TOWN OF TERRY

P. O. BOX 327
TERRY, MISSISSIPPI 39170-0327
TELEPHONE 601-878-5521
FAX 601-878-9501

OFFICERS

RODERICK T. NICHOLSON
MAYOR

MARY R. SMITH
CLERK & TAX COLLECTOR

ALDERMEN

VIRGINIA BAILEY
BONNIE HOLLY
APRIL MILEY
CONNIE TAYLOR
DORIS YOUNG

Date: September 2, 2015

To: Board Members

Re: Veto Action for 5% Raises Proposed in FY 2016

After much reflection having heard from the Board of Aldermen, having heard from various of our staff, and much internal reflection, I have decided to veto the board's action for raises in the upcoming fiscal year.

I do understand and appreciate that the Board's purpose in proposing a 5% salary increase was to offset the Board's decision to have those employees who desired health insurance to independently obtain health insurance through the exchanges offered through the state. However, I feel that this action is not likely to yield intended results for the following reasons:

- A 5% raise may offset the majority of the insurance costs for basic coverage only. The salary increase will not make our employees whole. Comprehensive insurance coverage includes vision and dental benefits. This is vital to the employee's personal health maintenance as well as their utility to the town in their execution of their respective jobs.
- The best approach to health is prevention and addressing medical concerns earlier. This is best done through comprehensive health insurance.
- Even with a 5% increase, our salaries are not competitive with the industry. Because of this, several of our employees are likely to just take the additional funds and not obtain insurance. In effect, the town is passing off the town's issues with providing affordable insurance and making this the responsibility of our employees. In the end, we will have a workforce where the majority do not have insurance. Are we really doing our job by passing that responsibility on them?
- Having comprehensive health care benefits has and will go a long way toward attracting and retaining highly qualified and competent persons. Not providing these important benefits will likely result in a revolving door of employees in search of better work conditions and benefits.
- While it is a noble gesture to increase our workers' salaries and personnel, we need to ensure that we are adding sufficient improvements in the level of service provided by the town. These minimal increases in salary and personnel can often result in significant increase the town's burden in the form of additional payroll, social security, unemployment and other taxes. This is not a smart long-term strategy for the town or its employees.
- The health care insurance costs can be accommodated with no additional financial burden by the town. During this past fiscal year, our bookkeeping indicated that town did not exceed any areas of its budget. Health insurance costs were included in this budget. With more intensive oversight, I feel confident that better accountability to the Board as well as service to our employees can be simultaneously achieved.

Our employees work very hard every day in their service and dedication to the town. I would encourage you to show your support of our employees by agreeing to fund health care for our employees.

Sincerely,

Roderick T. Nicholson
Mayor, Town of Terry

Description: Mayor Nicholson's response letter to the Board of Aldermen denying health insurance benefits to the town's employees.
Source: Memo Authored by Mayor Rod Nicholson

114

Sentencing by Judge William Chapman

For the reasons that I have provided more in depth earlier, I entered a guilty plea to these embezzlement charges of $2,748.08 on November 23, 2015. I was taken into custody on this date and held in the Rankin County jail until December 7, 2015 for my sentencing. I absolutely could not believe it. During this time, I heard from my attorney, and he indicated that the pre-sentencing investigation recommended probation or some form of house arrest as I had no prior criminal record.

On December 7, 2015, Rankin County Judge William Chapman sentenced me to 40 years of time, with 30 years suspended, and 10 years to serve. All for $2,748.08 in credit card charges for repairs to my personal vehicle that I used in the conduct of business for the Town. And that I had already paid back even before I had been indicted. Present in Court were my wife and two of my sisters who reside in Texas. After the sentencing was read, I was immediately taken back into custody. I couldn't say thank you to my sisters for taking time out of their lives and work to come to Mississippi to support me. I wasn't allowed to contact my wife for four days after my sentencing.

This was the absolute worst experience of my adult life. Emotionally, it was worse than when I lost my mother. Until these charges, I had never been arrested for anything. At the time that I received my sentence before Judge Chapman, I literally thought that I would be in jail for the next 10 years.

Request for Reconsideration of Sentence

Four days after my sentencing, on Friday, December 11, 2015, I received a visit from my attorney. He indicated that he too was as shocked I was by the sentence and since that time had done some extensive research on sentencing for similar violations. He showed me a fairly extensive sentencing from various cases recently processed through the Rankin County Circuit Court system. Some involved other elected officials and some sentences were even handed down by Judge William Chapman. None of those persons with a similar profile as mine had received any jail time. Some of the cases involved amounts as much as $300K, and yet these persons only received probation.

My attorney also showed me a brief that he had filed just that day with the Rankin County Court. Further, my attorney indicated that I could not get Request for Sentencing Reconsideration Hearing until February 1, 2016. This meant that I had to remain in jail away from my family through the Thanksgiving, Christmas, and the New Year's holidays. In all the 30 years that I have been married and had a family, this would be the first time that I was away from them. It was a very sad time for my family and me.

IN THE CIRCUIT COURT OF RANKIN COUNTY, MISSISSIPPI

STATE OF MISSISSIPPI

v.

RODERICK NICHOLSON

CAUSE NUMBER 26671

MOTION FOR RECONSIDERATION

COMES NOW, Roderick Nicholson, by and thru counsel, and request this Honorable Court to reconsider the sentence imposed in this matter and would show unto the Court the following in support thereof:

1.   Roderick Nicholson was indicted for the offense of Embezzlement, five counts on March 26, 2015. The total amount of Embezzlement in the Indictment was approximately two thousand, seven hundred forty-eight dollars, and eight cents ($2,748.08).

2.   The Defendant attempted to enter a guilty plea with a recommendation from the Attorney General's Office on November 9, 2015. Said date was prior to the plea expiration deadline in the scheduling that the current counsel had received after he entered his appearance in this matter.

3.   The plea recommendation agreed upon by the Assistant Attorney General, the Defendant, and Defense Counsel required Defendant to serve 5 years of supervised probation and did not require the Defendant to serve any term of imprisonment.

4.   After being unable to complete the agreed upon plea with the recommendation from the State, the Defendant entered an "open" guilty plea before this Court on November 30, 2015.

1

5.   The Defendant appeared before this Court on December 7, 2015, and received a sentence of twenty years, with fifteen years suspended, and five years to serve on each count. Counts 1-2 were grouped together and ran concurrent. Counts 3-5 were grouped together and ran concurrent to each other, but consecutive to Counts 1-2, thereby creating a total term of imprisonment of ten years. Defendant was therefore sentenced to serve ten years of imprisonment for offenses totaling approximately $2,748.08.

6.   Defendant believes the sentence imposed may be a violation of the Eighth Amendment prohibition of cruel and unusual punishment as it significantly differs from what this Court and other courts in the State of Mississippi have imposed in cases involving a similar set of facts.

7.   The Mississippi Supreme Court has held that "where a sentence is 'grossly disproportionate' to the crime committed, the sentence is subject to attack on the grounds that it violates the Eight Amendment prohibition of cruel and unusual punishment. " *Wallace v. State*, 607 So.2d 1184, 188 (Miss. 1992).

8.   The principle that a punishment should be proportionate to the crime is deeply rooted and frequently repeated in common law jurisprudence. *Solem v. Helm*, 463 U.S. 277, 284 (1983). The Supreme Court has stated, "The constitutional principle of proportionality has been recognized explicitly in this Court..." *Id.* at 286. The Court articulated that "as a matter of principle that a criminal sentence must proportionate to the crime for which the defendant has been convicted." *Id.* at 290.

9.   In evaluating the proportionality of a sentence, the *Solem* Court defined a three prong test:

2

(a)   The gravity of the offense and the harshness of the penalty;

(b)   Comparison of the sentence with sentences imposed on other criminals in the same jurisdiction; and

(c)   Comparison of sentences imposed in other jurisdictions for commission of the same crime.

Id. at 292.

10.   The sentence imposed in the instant cause against Defendant Nicholson is vastly different from other sentences imposed for similar conduct in this judicial district. For example, Charles Lindsay, a former elected official, who was indicted for embezzling approximately $28,000, was allowed to enter the pretrial diversion program with the Rankin County District Attorney's office and his charges were eventually expunged. In another matter involving a non-public official, the defendant Krista Danielle Brown (Cause #2015-0196), was charged with embezzling an amount greater than $25,000.00. Defendant Brown was sentenced to five years' probation and was not required to serve a term of imprisonment. Additionally, in the case of the "Bassfield 6", six Bassfield Mississippi elected officials and employees received sentences requiring no prison time in Rankin County Circuit Court, even though the potential amount of loss to the city was over $300,000.

11.   The sentence imposed against Roderick Nicholson is not only greater than sentences normally imposed in this judicial district, but said sentence is greater than previously imposed throughout the State of Mississippi. *In State of Mississippi v Charles Gregory Davis,* Circuit Court of Desoto County, Cause #2012-1226, the Defendant was convicted at trial of Making a False Statement with

3

Intent to Defraud and Embezzlement by a Public Official, yet Defendant was only sentenced to a term of imprisonment of two and one/half (2 ½) years for both counts, which were ran concurrent. The restitution order in the case of Defendant Davis was in excess of $17,000.00, yet he only received a fraction of the time Defendant Nicholson was sentenced to serve.

12.   Additionally former Warren County Circuit Clerk Shelly Ashley-Palmertree was sentenced to a five year term of imprisonment for embezzling over $100,000.00 while she was in office. An amount that far exceeds that $2,748.08 contained in Defendant Nicholson's indictment, yet her prison term was half of that imposed by Defendant Nicholson.

13.   In the *State of Mississippi vs David Kweller*, a case handled in the Hinds County Circuit, Kweller was a public employee who embezzled over $23,000, yet he received one year house arrest.

14.   Yvette Yeager, a former state employee, embezzled over $85,155.65 from the City of Greenville, Mississippi, and was sentenced to two years house arrest in the Circuit Court of Washington County.

15.   A review of the website of the State Auditor's office and the Mississippi Attorney General's office indicates that individuals who have been charged with embezzlement involving an amount similar to that of Defendant Nicholson normally receive non-adjudicated probation or a suspended sentence, even those handled in the Circuit Court of Rankin County.

WHEREFORE, PREMISES CONSIDERED, for the reasons listed above and others to be shown at the hearing in this matter, Defendant respectfully the Court vacate the sentence previously imposed in this matter.

4

Respectfully submitted,
RODERICK NICHOLSON

_____
Damon R. Stevenson

Damon R. Stevenson MSB 102945
STEVENSON LEGAL GROUP PLLC
P.O. Box 1922
Jackson, MS. 39255-1922
(769) 251-0207
(601) 608-7872
Damon.steven@gmail.com

6

Description: Request for Sentencing Reconsideration
Filed with Rankin County Circuit Court.
Source: Damon R. Stevenson, Attorney

On February 1, 2016 my attorney and I met back before Rankin County Circuit Court Judge William Chapman for sentencing reconsideration of this case. I had dealt with so much frustration and disappointment regarding this entire matter that I had no real expectation that I would get any reconsideration.

However, something was different on this date. Unlike on December 7, 2015 where there were all kinds of news media present to document and broadcast the case, there was none of that at my sentencing reconsideration hearing. I don't think that there was anyone even from the newspapers there to report on this matter. My wife was present, but the Courtroom was practically empty. Also, Judge Chapman seemed to have a different attitude and demeanor. I can't remember all that he said, but this time he seemed more compassionate and less angry. I believe that he was even complimentary of some of my accomplishments as Mayor. I was truly surprised that he amended my sentence to one year house arrest.

I wouldn't learn until after I had been back at home that a number of persons made a bunch of telephone calls, wrote letters, called the news and television media and otherwise lobbied on my behalf. I don't know for sure, but I do think that these efforts may have made a difference. Some of these persons I am aware of, and others I may never know. And to all of them, and to God, I thank you from the bottom of my heart.

Epilogue

I usually arise early each day, and I like to have this brief time alone for meditation and prayer. There is not one day that goes by that I don't ask thanksgiving to God for seeing fit to allow me to be reunited with my family. I am very sincere in this prayer. I am indeed very glad to be reunited with my family.

However, the damage has already been done to my reputation and professional career. By entering the guilty plea, I automatically had to give up my position as Mayor. That was the goal of my political adversaries all along: To get me removed from the position of Mayor at any cost. I have said this before, but I naively thought that being Mayor in a small town would never involve the hard ball tactics that you commonly read and hear about in larger metropolitan areas. I often wonder did the people who plotted this really intend for me to go to jail and otherwise be publicly maligned and humiliated as I have. Did they care? Indeed, I may never know.

And despite the tactics employed by my local political adversaries, would the State of Mississippi have pursued and handled this case as they did had I been white instead of African American? I highly doubt it. I do believe in God, and I think that all involved will eventually have their day of atonement before Him. The only thing that has given me the strength to deal with this is the knowledge that there are many persons in the State of Mississippi (mainly African American) who have suffered as much as I have if not more. As painful as this has been for me, I am no more immune from suffering than anyone else.

I have spent more than $20K in legal fees to protect and defend myself in a part-time Mayor position that paid less than $500/month after taxes. Prior to all this political drama, I was employed as a Civil Engineer with the federal government for 29-1/2 years with a spotless record of distinguished service. As a result of the publicity surrounding this case, I am no longer employed in my federal job.

However, I would like to say that there are some very good people from all walks of life here in this state. But Mississippi needs to be honest with how historically abusive she has been (and in many ways continues to be) to the African American. There are times that I have cursed myself for staying here. I ask myself whether the good outweighs the bad by remaining here in this state. Sometimes, I honestly don't know.

I am reminded of the African American cult movie classic, "The Color Purple", where Celie says to Mister: "Until you do right by me, everything you even think about is going to fail!" In this analogy, Celie represents the African Americans of Mississippi, and Mister represents the white racist powerbrokers in the State of Mississippi. I truly hope that the good people of all walks of life in this state will prevail and not rest until a much needed change in Mississippi is achieved.

As of the conclusion of this memoir, I do not have any solid prospects for gainful employment. However, I don't plan for this to be the end of Rod Nicholson. I thank God that I have my health, I still have a good mind, and I want to continue to be productive, not be a burden, and continue to make a positive contribution somehow. I served as Mayor for more than ten years, and I worked as a Civil Engineer for more than thirty years. I am cautiously optimistic that I still have a skill set and have something valuable to offer to the marketplace in order to support my family and myself.

On February 1, 2016, Rankin County Circuit Court Judge William Chapman amended my 40-year (suspending 30 years with 10 years to serve) sentence to one (1) year of house arrest. According the MDOC, barring no problems during my house arrest, I would be eligible for parole on November 22, 2016.

There have been problems in the interpretation of this sentence almost from the beginning. My attorney had indicated to me that I should have served only three (3) months considering that I already was incarcerated for 2-1/2 months prior, and according to the sentencing guidelines under Mississippi HB 485, this offense qualified for parole after serving 25% of the sentence time (in this case 3 months). However, one could also argue that granting of parole is a privilege not a right and therefore parole is not an automatic expectation.

However, the Commissioner of the MS Department of Corrections apparently didn't see it that way. I had been told that the 2-1/2 months that I spent incarcerated would be taken off of my probation time. The State of Mississippi again has shown how punitive they can be especially to African Americans.

In an effort to move on from this horrific experience and move my life forward, I have submitted applications for civil engineering jobs both within and outside of the State of Mississippi. And I have received a few serious requests from out of state to appear for an interview. Unfortunately, while I was on house arrest, the MS Department of Corrections would not permit me to travel out of state for a job interview and/or receive required out of state pre-employment job training. Does this make sense to deny an able bodied, educated man an opportunity to provide for his family? Who will feed, clothe, shelter, and otherwise provide for my family if I don't? Certainly not the State of Mississippi.

On June 23, 2016, I was advised by the MS Department of Corrections that my house rest was concluded five months early and that I was placed on a five-year parole. I am grateful to have a greater degree of freedom. However, I still contend that these charges were bogus and the sentence was excessive and extremely punitive. I have been personally told by administrators within the correction system that they feel that my case is one of the more unfair sentences that they have seen in a long time. Even by Mississippi standards.

As a convicted felon, I can no longer hold a federal job, in some cases, I am no longer able to vote, and I cannot possess a firearm to defend my family and myself. My goal is to have these charges expunged from my record and have my full rights and privileges as a citizen restored. My existence has posed no threat to any person or community in the past nor do I expect my existence to pose a threat to any person or community in the future.

I'd like to share with you a dream that my daughter Vanessa shared with me. In her dream, her late paternal grandmother (my mother) appeared before her. In my daughter's dream, my mother told her: "Tell June (that was my nickname growing up) that these people thought they had buried him. However, they didn't realize that he was a seed. Please give this message to your father, Vanessa." And then my mother vanished.

My interpretation of my daughter's dream is that Mama meant to relay to me to not give up. I don't know what the future holds for me. But I do not plan for this to be the end of Roderick T. Nicholson. Mama, I don't plan on giving up.

I do hope that my story can be of some interest, comfort, education, or inspiration to another human being on this earth. I felt so compelled to write my memoirs of this period of time in my life. I am grateful to be able to share my experiences with the reader.

Through this memoir, I had to acknowledge and respond to all the negativity that seemed to surround the last year and a half of my administration as Mayor of the Town of Terry, MS. However, I am cautiously optimistic that time will reflect more positively than negatively upon my more than ten year administration as the first African American Mayor of the Town of Terry MS. There is much that we have to be proud of:

- Construction of an award winning Terry City Hall ($300K)
- Construction of the Ella Bess Austin-Terry Public Library ($450K)
- The first improvement (reduction) in the town's fire insurance rating in almost 50 years
- The construction of the new, centrally located fire station building ($275K)
- Construction of a new public works building ($275K)
- Establishment of Hope Credit Union when Regions Bank closed its Terry Branch, thus allowing the community to continue to have banking services.
- Major Paving Projects (through grants secured for the town):
  - Cunningham Avenue ($400K)
  - Utica Street ($375K)
  - Morgan Drive ($100K)
  - Southfork Estates subdivision ($175K)
- Significant improvements in and expansion of the town's water and sewer infrastructure:
  - NE Terry Sewer Expansion Project ($1.2 million)
  - Old Highway 51 Sewer Project ($500K)

- ° Comprehensive City-Wide Water Infrastructure Expansion Project ($600K)
- ° Upgraded Terry Water Service rating to perfect (5.0/5.0) five years in a row
- ° Major rehabilitation of town's water tank to extend tank's useful life and appearance without increasing taxes ($300K)
- ° Major Improvements in appearance of Village Square Park including a $20K grant for playground equipment
- Annexation of prime land to enhance the town's potential for economic development and future growth
- Working with the business community to meet the community's needs and demands for quality, modern housing (Cedarstone, Terry Park, Southfork Estates, and Sage Hill subdivisions)
- Economic development for the town that began in earnest with the establishment of Skinner's (a full-service General Motors automobile dealership) and Fred's Super Dollar Store (retail) in Terry.

Finally, I hope that I will be remembered as someone who saw the glass as half full rather than half empty, as someone who truly understood and embraced the importance and benefits of diversity by actively engaging all the town's demographics (black, white, young, old, etc.) as this I believe is the only way that we can truly move our community and state forward. I want to thank the reader for the opportunity to share my memoirs with you. I do hope that you have found them interesting, informative, and educational about the joys and burdens of living and dreaming in Mississippi.

-**RTN**

Printed in the United States
By Bookmasters